Study Guide for Book Clubs: A Gentleman in Moscow

KATHRYN COPE

CONTENTS

INTRODUCTION

There are few things more rewarding than getting together with a group of like-minded people and discussing a good book. Book club meetings, at their best, are vibrant, passionate affairs. Each member will bring along a different perspective and ideally there will be heated debate.

A surprising number of book club members, however, report that their meetings have been a disappointment. Even though their group loved the particular book they were discussing, they could think of astonishingly little to say about it. Failing to find interesting discussion angles for a book is the single most common reason for book group discussions to fall flat. Most book groups only meet once a month and a lacklustre meeting is frustrating for everyone.

Study Guides for Book Clubs were born out of a passion for reading groups. Packed with information, they take the hard work out of preparing for a meeting and ensure that your book group discussions never run dry. How you choose to use the guides is entirely up to you. The author biography, historical, and style sections provide useful background information which may be interesting to share with your group at the beginning of your meeting. The all-important list of discussion questions, which will probably form the core of your meeting, can be found towards the end of this guide. To support your responses to the discussion questions, you may find it helpful to refer to the 'Themes' and 'Character' sections.

A detailed plot synopsis is provided as an aide-memoire if you need to recap on the finer points of the plot. There is also a quick quiz - a fun way to test your knowledge and bring your discussion to a close. Finally, if this was a book that you particularly enjoyed, the guide concludes with a list of books similar in style or subject matter.

Be warned, this guide contains spoilers. Please do not be tempted to read it before you have read the original novel as plot surprises will be well and truly ruined.

Kathryn Cope, 2017

AMOR TOWLES

Amor Towles was born in 1964 and raised in Boston, USA. After graduating from Yale University, he received an MA in English from Stanford University. His debut novel, *The Rules of Civility*, was published in 2011. Set in the 1930s, it tells the rags-to-riches story of Katey Kontent, a girl from the Bronx who, thanks to a chance encounter, reinvents herself as a lady of Manhattan high society. Praised for its stylish tone, witty dialogue and vivid evocation of historical period, *The Rules of Civility* marked Towles out as an exciting literary talent, giving him the courage to give up a career in finance in order to write full-time.

Towles' second novel, *A Gentleman in Moscow*, combined the author's attraction to the historical period of the 1920s and 1930s with his interest in Russian literature and culture. It was also inspired by the many hotels he visited across the world when working in the investment business. After staying in the same hotel in Geneva for eight years in a row and recognising some of the guests from previous stays, the author began to imagine a character forced to live in a hotel for the rest of his life.

Towles lives in Manhattan with his wife and two children.

PLOT SYNOPSIS

The book begins with a poem: 'Where Is It Now?' by Count Rostov. This is followed by a court transcript recounting the proceedings of a meeting of the Emergency Committee of the People's Commissariat for Internal Affairs in the Kremlin. The document details the questioning of Count Alexander Rostov. The Count denies that he returned to Russia from Paris to fight either for or against the Revolution. Nevertheless, his unapologetic manner antagonises his questioners. The Committee conclude that, although the Count's famous poem 'Where Is It Now?' seemed to show sympathy with the revolutionary cause he has now become a typically corrupt aristocrat. They conclude that he will be placed under house arrest at the Hotel Metropol where he currently resides. If he ever steps outside its doors he will be shot.

BOOK ONE

1922: An Ambassador

Rostov is escorted back to the hotel. The officers tell him that he will no longer be staying in Suite 317: a grand room with views of Theatre Square. Instead he is shown to a tiny attic room and told that he can transfer whatever belongings he can fit in the small space. The Count chooses items largely based on their sentimental value. These include a painting of his sister, Helena, his father's twice-tolling clock, his grandmother's opera glasses and a desk inherited from his godfather, the Grand Duke Demidov. The desk has the added advantage of gold coins concealed inside its legs. Andrey, the maître d' of the hotel restaurant; Vasily, the concierge, and Marina, the hotel seamstress, visit the Count to express their relief that he has returned from the Kremlin alive. Rostov invites them in to his cramped new quarters to celebrate.

From the narrator we learn what the Count failed to tell the

Committee – that he returned to Russia from Paris to ensure his grandmother's safe exile after the execution of Tsar Nicholas II. Convincing the Countess to leave Idlehour (their family estate) and escape abroad, the Count closed up the great house and set off for Moscow with the finest of the Rostovs' furniture in a single wagon.

An Anglican Ashore

The Count realises that his usual routines (visits to the Conservatory or Alexander Gardens, lunch at the Jockey Club, and mornings spent in his favourite bakery) will no longer be possible under the terms of his house arrest. In return for a gold coin, he asks a Greek moneylender to deliver three notes for him in Moscow. He fills the time until dinner by conversing with the hotel's one-eyed cat and starting to read his father's copy of *The Essays of Montaigne*.

The Count has dinner at the Boyarsky, the hotel's top-class restaurant. In the aftermath of the Revolution there has been an economic and agricultural crisis and culinary ingredients are hard to come by. Luckily, the hotel's chef, Emile, displays genius in his ability to improvise with cheap ingredients. Rostov successfully identifies the sage-like herb in his dish as nettle – much to the fiery chef's frustration. When the Count returns to his room, delivery boys arrive with the fruit of the notes he sent: luxurious bed linen, fine soap and a mille-feuille from his favourite bakery.

An Appointment

Time drags as the Count struggles to concentrate on Montaigne's essays. At noon he is relieved to escape for his weekly appointment with Yaroslav Yaroslavl, the hotel barber. Yaroslavl's barber shop is an oasis of old-world charm, epitomised by his glass cabinet displaying tonics, soaps and a mysterious bottle described as 'the Fountain of Youth'. The relaxing experience is rudely interrupted, however, when a waiting customer accuses Count Rostov of jumping the queue. Enraged, the man cuts off one side of the Count's luxuriant moustache and storms off. Unflustered, the Count asks for a clean shave.

An Acquaintanceship

Count Rostov dines in the Piazza, the second restaurant in the Hotel Metropol. Previously bustling before the war, the Count observes that the restaurant is nearly empty. Rostov also notes that the man serving him (who resembles a bishop chess piece due to his narrow head and superior manner) is surprisingly incompetent. Recommending an entirely inappropriate wine to complement his meal, 'the Bishop' then fails to deliver the Count's preferred vintage to his table. Rostov's meal is further disrupted when a young girl joins him after impertinently asking him where his moustaches went. Nina Kulikova, the nine-year-old daughter of a Ukrainian bureaucrat, then asks the Count to tell her everything he knows about the lives of princesses. When the conversation turns to dueling, the Count tells Nina that his godfather took part in a duel when he was staying at the Hotel Metropol. At the time, the hotel manager kept a handy pair of pistols hidden in his office for feuding guests.

Anyway …

Five days later, the Count accepts a formal invitation to tea with Nina. When she asks him to tell her the "rules of being a princess" the Count emphasises the importance of manners, posture and respect for elders. To illustrate his point, he tells the story of Princess Golitsyn who bypasses a grand party in order to give a poor old woman a lift to her son's home and politely take tea with the woman's family. Nina tells the Count that she will work on her manners but will never say thank you when offered something she hasn't asked for.

Around and About

Nina rescues the Count from boredom by taking him on regular 'excursions' around the hotel. After living in the hotel for ten months, she is familiar with all the hidden parts of the Metropol including the basement, which houses the boiler room, the furnace and lost property. When the Count discovers a locked blue door in the basement Nina reveals that she carries a hotel passkey on a chain around her neck. They open the door to find a storeroom housing the hotel's silver service. Nina and the Count also use the key to let themselves in to each of the hotel rooms when the occupants are out. After revisiting Suite 317, the Count's attic room seems smaller than ever. Working on a hunch that the back of his wardrobe may be built into an old doorframe, he breaks through the back and finds himself in the closet of the room next door. Delighted, the Count furnishes this secret room as a study. Giving up on Montaigne, he begins to reread his favourite novel, *Anna Karenina*.

An Assembly

One of Nina's favourite activities is to hide behind the ballroom balcony and spy on the Bolshevik Assemblies that frequently take place there. The Count accompanies her to observe the Second Meeting of the First Congress of the Moscow Branch of the All-Russian Union of Railway Workers. In the undignified process of hunching down behind the balcony the Count splits the seam of his pants for a second time, necessitating another visit to seamstress Marina.

Later, the Count is summoned by Mr. Halecki, the hotel manager. Halecki apologetically tells Rostov that members of his staff are no longer permitted to address him as "Your Excellency". When Halecki leaves the room at an urgent summons from the Desk Manager, Arkady, Count Rostov opens a secret panel in the wall and finds that dueling pistols are still hidden there.

Archaeologies

The Count receives a surprise visit from his friend, Mikhail Fyodorovich Mindich (otherwise known as Mishka). Honouring a Rostov family tradition, Mishka produces a bottle of Châteauneuf-du-Pape and announces that he has come to toast the 10th anniversary of the Grand Duke's death. Mishka is also in Moscow to attend the Russian Association of Proletarian Writers. Count' Rostov's friend expresses excitement at the progress he believes post-revolutionary Russia will enjoy and anticipates an end to oppression and ignorance.

Advent

In the Piazza the Count meets Nina, who is going home for Christmas and then starting school in January. As a Christmas gift he presents her with his grandmother's opera glasses. In return, Nina gives him a wrapped package but instructs him not to open it until midnight strikes. At a nearby table the Count observes a romantic young couple. Despairing when he sees the Bishop recommend an expensive and inappropriate wine for the couple's meal, Rostov intervenes with his own suggestion.

Back in his room, the Count waits for the strike of twelve to open Nina's gift. Inside are boxes within boxes. The final and smallest one contains the hotel passkey.

In an aside, the narrator informs us that, in four years' time, the Count will be climbing the hotel roof in order to throw himself off.

BOOK TWO

1923: An Actress, an Apparition, an Apiary

On the first anniversary of his house arrest, the Count notices a "willowy" woman in the lobby. The woman's striking appearance is enhanced by the two borzois she has on a leash. When the one-eyed cat makes an appearance and taunts the dogs, chaos ensues. As the attractive woman clearly has no control over her pets, the Count whistles the dogs to heel. When the woman blames her dogs for their bad behaviour, the Count suggests it is their handler that is the problem. Later, he sees the woman in the hotel bar accompanied by a "round-faced" balding man.

The Count receives a brief visit from Mishka, who is again attending a Congress of the Russian Association of Proletarian Writers. Mishka confides that he has fallen in love with a fellow committee member, Katerina Litvinova, and hurries off. Audrius, the bartender of the hotel, then gives the Count a note from the woman with the borzois asking for "a second chance at a first impression". Audrius tells Count Rostov that the note's sender is Anna Urbanova, a movie star.

When the Count arrives at Anna's suite he discovers that she has ordered a meal for two from room service. Particularly impressed by the way she debones and serves their sea bass, he reassesses his first, unfavourable impression of her. Anna tells the Count that she learned to fillet fish from her father, who was a fisherman. In return, the Count tells her about his childhood in Nizhny Novgorod, where he claims apples of every colour and size grew. Anna wastes no time in seducing the Count but at one in the morning asks him to leave and draw the curtains as he goes. The Count does as he is instructed and also hangs Anna's discarded blouse on a clothes hanger on the way out. He goes to the elevator feeling like a ghost. Inside he meets the one-eyed cat who looks at him sternly.

On the way back to his room, the Count spots a ladder leading to an open roof hatch. On the hotel roof he meets Abram, one of the hotel handymen. Abram invites Count Rostov to join him for coffee and to try the honey from the bees he keeps in crates on the roof. The honey tastes of the lilacs of the Alexander Gardens which are currently blooming, reminding the Count of the many happy afternoons he spent there. Abram tells him that in a few weeks' time their honey will taste of the cherry trees from the Garden Ring. As they talk, the two men discover that they were both raised in Nizhny Novgorod, where apple blossoms flourish.

Addendum

Anna leaves the Metropol and travels back to St. Petersburg. In the weeks that follow she feels increasingly furious when she pictures Count Rostov hanging her blouse up before leaving her room. She begins to leave her clothes on the floor at the end of each day and instructs her staff not to pick them up. After two weeks, Olga, Anna's dresser, threatens to spank her employer if she doesn't pick her clothes up. Anna defiantly throws her clothes out of the window but at two in the morning sneaks out into the street to pick them up.

1924: Anonymity

The Count continues to feel that Anna has cast a spell of invisibility on him, as other people no longer seem to notice his presence. He seeks out Nina but she is busy attempting to solve mathematical conundrums. Mishka then cancels a dinner arrangement with the Count as Katerina is ill and he is returning to

St. Petersburg to be with her.

Dining alone in the Boyarsky, the Count is dismayed to be served by the Bishop who informs him that there are only two choices of wine - red or white. Count Rostov asks to speak to Andrey who explains that the Bishop has been promoted from the Piazza, as he clearly has an influential friend in the Communist Party. Andrey takes the Count down to the wine cellar to show him that all the labels have been removed from the bottles. He tells him the restaurant's extensive wine list has been judged to be at odds with revolutionary ideals after an anonymous complaint (presumably from the Bishop). The Count recalls the moment when he contradicted the Bishop's wine recommendation to a young couple and realises that this is the source of his grievance. He scans the thousands of bottles on the wine racks until he identifies a Châteauneuf-du-Pape by the two crossed keys embossed on the glass. He takes the bottle, resolving that on the 22 June 1926 he will commemorate the tenth anniversary of his sister's death by drinking it and then dying.

1926: Adieu

Life at the hotel continues to move on without Count Rostov. Staff members leave and increasingly inexperienced substitutes take their place; Nina is soon to move to a large apartment for Party officials with her father; and even the bees on the roof have left their hives. Having paid all his accounts and left a letter for Mishka and instructions for the undertaker, the Count plans to kill himself at the stroke of midnight.

As Count Rostov enjoys a final nightcap in the Shalyapin (the Metropol's American-style bar), he overhears a conversation between a British man and a German. While the Brit extolls the merits of Russia, the German is dismissive, claiming that vodka is the only thing of worth that Russia has ever produced. When the German offers to buy a glass of vodka for anyone who can name three other notable Russian attributes, the Count accepts the challenge on the proviso that, if he succeeds, they will all drink a glass of vodka together. The Count lists his first Russian great as Chekov and Tolstoy, arguing that both are masters of their literary form. His second is the first scene of Tchaikovsky's *The Nutcracker* which captures the very essence of Christmas. For his third Russian great the Count signals a waiter who brings in a tray of caviar. The German admits defeat and becomes intoxicated on vodka while Count Rostov chats to the British man, Charles Abernethy.

When Charles asks the Count why he left Russia only to return again, Rostov explains that, in 1913, he attended the twenty-first birthday celebrations of Princess Novobackzky. On the way to the party, his carriage was run off the road by the galloping troika of an arrogant young officer of the Hussars, Lieutenant Pulonov. Once at the party, the Count got his own back by beating Pulonov at cards and then romancing the Princess while his rival was distracted by the fine wine and food. Months later, however, Pulonov took his revenge by courting the Count's sister, Helena, and then deliberately breaking her heart. The Count shot Pulonov and although the lieutenant survived, the resulting injury left him with a lame right arm, meaning he had to give up his commission in the Hussars. After Pulonov's father filed a complaint, the Count's grandmother sent him to Paris to avoid prosecution. When the war broke out, however, Pulonov insisted upon returning to the Hussars to lead his regiment and, as a result of his lame arm, was killed with a bayonet.

Charles tries to reassure Count Rostov that he cannot take full responsibility for Pulonov's death. The Count insists that he was responsible for the chain of events that led to his sister's humiliation. He also explains that, if he had not been exiled to Paris for shooting Pulonov, he would have been at his sister's side when she died of scarlet fever.

The Count goes up to the hotel roof. He uncorks the Châteauneuf-du-Pape and is about to throw himself to his death when he is interrupted by Abram. The excited old man tells him that his bees have returned and insists that he should taste their honey. The Count identifies the taste of apple-blossom in the honey and realises that the bees have returned from Nizhny Novgorod, more than a hundred miles away. Abram suggests that, over the years, the bees have been listening to their childhood tales of Nizhny Novgorod and resolved to visit there. The Count returns to his room and retrieves the instructions he has left for the undertaker.

BOOK THREE

1930

As the Count relishes the distinct flavours of his breakfast, someone slips an envelope under his door.

Arachne's Art

In the past four years a number of significant historical changes have taken place in Russia. The country's leader, Stalin, has launched his five-year-plan which aims to make Russia a great power by collectivizing farming and increasing industrial output. He has also introduced Article 58 of the Criminal Code, effectively criminalising any activities judged to be counter to the Party's ideals.

Changes have also taken place in the Metropol, which is once again a bustling hotel. The Assemblies that once took place in the ballroom have been replaced by dinners of state for the Communist Party and the Bishop has been promoted to assistant manager. Wine labels have also been reintroduced after a member of the Central Committee was frustrated to find he couldn't order a bottle of Bordeaux for the French ambassador.

Now headwaiter of the Boyarsky, the Count finds his talents are put to good use in recommending suitable wines for every budget and ensuring that members of the Politburo are allocated appropriate tables. Each day he meets with Emile and Andrey to discuss restaurant business and taste the day's specials. At the end of the present meeting, the Count reveals that the envelope discretely slipped under his door earlier contains saffron.

Count Rostov has received a letter from Mishka, who moved to Kiev with Katerina four years previously. Katerina has left him for another man, however, and Mishka has now returned to St. Petersburg to lose himself in his work. As the Count starts to read his friend's letter he observes a group of young people in the lobby who are clearly members of the Komsomol (a youth organisation of the Communist Party). When one of the young men eagerly fetches the coat of the blonde woman and she fails to thank him, he recognises Nina. Nina tells Count Rostov they are leaving for the Kady District to help collectivize the region. She earnestly expresses her faith that the five-year-plan will serve the common good of the people.

Marina has taught Count Rostov how to repair his own clothes and they often sit and sew companionably together. That afternoon, the Count describes his encounter with Nina to Marina and tells her that he fears Nina's convictions are preventing her from enjoying her youth. At 4 p.m. the Count goes to Suite 311 where Anna Urbanova is waiting for him in the bedroom.

An Afternoon Assignation

The narrator reveals that Anna and Count Rostov resumed their acquaintanceship in 1928 and describes the trajectory of events that brought them together again.

At the beginning of her acting career, Anna was the ingénue of a film director whose films were approved of by the government. When the director's films fell out of favour, however, so did Anna. This fall from grace was hastened by the introduction of the talking picture for which Anna's husky voice was deemed inappropriate. At the age of 29 Anna became a 'has-been' and her luxuriously furnished mansion was confiscated.

Count Rostov first saw Anna again in 1928 as she met a young director at the Metropol. After having dinner with her, the director declined an invitation to Anna's suite, leaving her humiliated. The Count, however, was more than happy to accept where the director had declined.

After this, Anna became a regular guest at the hotel, meeting up with different directors in the hope of securing small character roles but never again asking them up for a nightcap. Her persistence paid off when Panteleimon Nachevko (her round-faced admirer) saw her in one of these roles. Having risen to a senior role in the Ministry of Culture, Nachevko used his influence to resuscitate Anna's career. Although once again a star with a grand house, Anna has been humbled by her fall from grace. She admits to the Count that her father was a peasant, not a fisherman, and she learned to debone fish when she worked in a tavern.

An Alliance

Half-way through service at the Boyarsky the Count is asked to attend a private function in the Yellow Room. The function room is guarded by an intimidating security guard and inside is a middle-aged man with a distinctive scar above his left ear. The man introduces himself as Osip Ivanovich Glebnikov, former colonel of the Red Army, and asks the Count to join him.

Osip explains that Russia is at a point where it has the potential to become a major world power. To do so, however, it is vital to establish diplomatic relationships with France, Britain and America. In order to facilitate these relationships, Osip believes he must learn the countries' languages and understand their society and cultures. He asks the Count to dine with him once a month to educate him in these matters.

Absinthe

For three years, Emile, Andrey and the Count have secretly planned to get hold of the fifteen ingredients of bouillabaisse. Anna has used her influence to acquire the saffron – a particularly rare ingredient at a time of food shortages. The Count acquires the final ingredient (a glass of absinthe) from the bar and meets Andrey and Emile in the kitchen. Their long-awaited meal seems to be endangered when the Bishop arrives to ask them why they are congregating in the kitchen at night. When Emile threatens the Bishop with a celery stalk, however, the assistant manager hurries away, mistaking the celery for the chef's infamous chopping knife. The three men settle down to eat and talk in the early hours of the morning. Andrey reveals that he first arrived in Moscow as a member of a travelling circus and demonstrates his superb juggling skills with oranges and knives.

After the meal the Count realises that he has lost the half-read letter he received from Mishka. He fails to find it and the narrator reveals the letter has fallen between the Count's bookcase and the wall. For this reason, he doesn't discover that the poem Mishka quoted on the first page was not written by his friend but by Vladimir Mayakovsy, "poet laureate of the Revolution" who has shot himself through the heart.

Addendum

As an excited Nina boards a train to Ivanovo, the narrator explains why her mission is doomed to end in disillusionment. As part of Stalin's five-year plan, industry grew in the cities of Russia, with the building of new power stations, steel mills and factories. To meet the increased demand for food in the country's growing industrial areas, it was also necessary for rural areas to increase grain production. To achieve this aim, a million kulaks (independent farmers) were forced to give up their farms to collectivization. While collectivization was heralded as a more efficient agricultural system, a lack of tractors and farming know-how, combined with bad weather conditions, led to famine and the starvation of millions of Ukrainian peasants. Meanwhile, the Russian government kept the plight of their rural citizens quiet.

1938: An Arrival

The narrator summarises the grim realities of life in 1930s Russia. The 1932 famine led to the mass migration of peasants to the cities which, in turn, led to overcrowding and shortages of essentials. Industrial workers were worked hard and paid badly, while artists were constrained by censorship and churches were burned to the ground.

Meanwhile, Nina unexpectedly arrives at the Metropol. She tells the Count that Leo, her husband, has been arrested and sentenced to five years of corrective labour in Sevvostlag. Nina plans to follow her husband but explains that she needs Count Rostov to look after her daughter, Sofia. She promises that she will return for Sofia once she has found work and a place to live.

Adjustments

The Count finds that time drags as his attempts to amuse six-year-old Sofia fall flat. When Sofia suggests that his clock must be broken, as it does not chime every hour, Count Rostov explains that it is a unique twice-tolling clock, commissioned by his father to strike only on the hours of noon and midnight. The Count's stories of life at Idlehour finally succeed in sparking Sofia's interest.

Ascending, Alighting

With Sofia in tow, the Count finds it hard to juggle the various demands of his day. He is uncharacteristically late for an assignation with Anna and, during a meeting with Osip, he is forced to confess that he hasn't had time to read the text they are discussing.

To complicate matters further, an agitated Mishka arrives in Moscow a day earlier than expected. For several years he has been working on a volume of Anton Chekhov's letters, commissioned by an old acquaintance, Victor Shalamov. He furiously tells the Count, however, that Shalamov has asked him to remove a section in one of Chekov's letters which compares Russian bread unfavourably with the "amazing" bread to be had in Berlin. The Count advises Mishka to go back to his hotel to sleep on the matter and assures him that they will meet again the next day.

As there is insufficient room for another mattress, the Count constructs bunk beds to accommodate Sofia. Worried about Mishka, Nina and the certainty that someone will report Sofia's presence at the hotel to the authorities, he struggles to get to sleep.

The next day, Mishka walks through Moscow and sees that the famous statue of Gogol (one of his literary heroes) has been replaced by an effigy of Gorky. Realising that those poets who he predicted would forge a new poetry have all been silenced, he angrily confronts Shalamov in a conference. Shortly afterwards, the authorities are told of Mishka's actions and, in March 1939, he is exiled to Siberia. Meanwhile, we learn that Nina never returned to Moscow and the Count's attempts to discover her whereabouts proved fruitless. As the Count feared, within two weeks of Sofia's arrival, someone reports her presence at the hotel to the Kremlin. When it is discovered that one of the Count's associates is an actress who is rumoured to be the mistress of a 'round-faced' member of the Politburo, however, no action is taken, as Sofia is presumed to be the Commissar's illegitimate daughter.

Addendum

Sofia wakes the Count in the middle of the night to tell him that she left her dolly in Marina's room.

1946

A ragged figure hobbles past the landmarks of the Soviet Union's recent history in the streets of Moscow. The "decommissioned tanks" he passes in front of the Kremlin celebrate the fact that Moscow escaped invasion during World War II (although one million Soviet lives were still lost). The figure also passes queues of people visiting the tomb of Lenin (who died over twenty years earlier) and the spot where Kazan Cathedral stood before it was burned to the ground. At Theatre Square, however, the man marvels at how many of the "old facades" remain standing before entering the hotel through the back entrance.

Antics, Antitheses, an Accident

The Bishop, who is now the hotel manager, questions the Count about an incident that took place on the fourth floor landing that morning. Count Rostov admits that he observed the incident, in which three geese ran amok among the hotel guests, but says he has no idea how the birds escaped from the Boyarsky pantry. The Count is indignant at the implication that thirteen-year-old Sofia may be responsible for the incident, although he privately acknowledges that she has a "playful streak". This is illustrated in a private game she has engineered with the Count. Often to be seen sitting studiously with a book, Sofia will then race to wherever the Count is headed and demurely wait for his arrival, as if she has been there all along.

As Count Rostov, Emile and Andrey express outrage at the Bishop's insinuation (despite the tell-tale feathers in the dumbwaiter), a ragged figure enters the kitchen. The Count barely recognises Mishka, whose appearance has been ravaged by eight years of hard labour. Mishka reveals that he has been issued with a Minus Six preventing him from setting foot in Moscow but has borrowed a friend's passport to enable him to visit.

Osip and Count Rostov still meet regularly for their educational discussions. While he generally enjoys their debates, the Count is troubled by Osip's suggestion that it is Russia's ability to unsentimentally throw off the past which will make it a great nation. The idea particularly concerns him as it echoes Mishka's belief that one of the defining characteristics of Russia is its willingness to destroy the great things it has created. In the hotel bar, the Count discusses this theory with Richard Vanderwhile, the aide-de-camp of an American general. Vanderwhile puts forward an alternative theory - that "grand things persist."

On leaving the bar, the Count sees Sofia sitting demurely in the lobby and senses that she is about to race up to their room before him. He sprints up the stairs, grabs Montaigne and sits in his chair waiting, but she doesn't arrive. Rostov is puzzled until a chambermaid bursts in to tell him that Sofia has fallen on the service stair.

The Count finds Sofia unconscious with a head injury, carries her outside and hires a taxi to St. Anselm's Hospital. When they reach the hospital, however, it is clear from the building's run-down state that it has been superseded by a more modern hospital elsewhere in Moscow.

Sofia's injury requires surgery and an inexperienced intern is about to operate on her when Dr. Lazovsky, the best surgeon in the city, arrives and insists that he will operate on Sofia. The operation is a success and afterwards the Count is astonished to find Dr. Lazovsky quietly conferring with Osip. Osip tells the Count that it has been a pleasure to repay his years of service and explains that Sofia will be taken to a superior hospital to recover, while he must return to the hotel before his absence is discovered. A baker's van waits at the back of the hospital to transport him back. On the journey the Count notices how much the streets he once knew have changed.

Safely back in his room, the Count finds a black leather case with a note from Richard Vanderwhile. Inside are a portable phonograph and a recording of Vladimir Horowitz playing Tchaikovsky's First Piano Concert at Carnegie Hall.

Addendum

Andrey regularly visits Sofia in hospital and reports back to Count Rostov on her progress. One of the rooms in the small apartment he shares with his wife is kept like a shrine to Ilya, their only child, who was killed in the Battle of Berlin.

BOOK FOUR

1950: Adagio, Andante, Allegro

The Count is horrified when he walks into the ballroom and finds

Sofia, who is now seventeen, sitting with Viktor Stepanovich, the conductor of the orchestra at the Piazza. Assuming the worst, the Count grabs Viktor by the lapels before Sofia can explain that the Conservatory trained musician has been teaching her to play the piano. When she plays a piece by Chopin the Count is overwhelmed by her talent.

Richard Vanderwhile now works for the State Department but, when he is in Moscow, still drops by the hotel to drink cocktails with the Count. During one of their discussions the Count tells Richard about 'the moths of Manchester': a species which changed its colour as disguise against the soot-covered trees of the industrial city.

1952: America

Over dinner the Count is approached by a professor of literature who asks Count Rostov to join him for a drink in Suite 317. On keeping the appointment, he finds Richard Vanderwhile waiting for him. Richard tells the Count that he has been promoted to a role at the American Embassy in Paris. He explains that, as Stalin is clearly nearing the end of his life, Russian politics are again likely to face a period of upheaval. With this in mind, the American government can offer generous rewards to 'friends' who are willing to pass on observations about the changing political climate. The Count makes it clear that he is not a spy and asks Richard not to speak of it again.

Nine months later, Stalin dies and Harrison Salisbury, a correspondent for *The New York Times,* watches from Suite 317 as Stalin's coffin passes by. As Richard Vanderwhile predicted, Stalin's death ushers in a new era of uncertainty for Russia. Of eight possible successors to Stalin, the joint favourites emerge as Premier Malenkov and General Secretary Nikita Khrushchev. Western powers hope for Malenkov, as he is known to be critical of nuclear arms.

1953: Apostles and Apostates

The Bishop introduces unpopular new procedures to the Boyarsky in which the entire process of a diner's meal must be recorded in triplicate to eliminate "discrepancies". The result of the lengthy procedure is that dishes arrive at the diners' tables cold.

Later, the Count sits up impatiently waiting for Sofia to return from a musical competition at the Grand Hall. Anna and Sofia eventually return triumphant but their celebrations are interrupted by the Bishop, accompanied by Ivan Frinovsky, the director of the Red October Youth Orchestra. Frinovsky announces that he wants Sofia to join his orchestra, which is based in Stalingrad, 600 miles away. The Count declares that Sofia is not interested but Frinovsky argues that the appointment has been rubber-stamped by the Undersecretary of Cultural Affairs. Anna intervenes, explaining that her friend, Panteleimon Nachevko (now Minister of Culture) has big plans for Sofia in Moscow.

Outside his room Count Rostov is intercepted by a woman who introduces herself as Katerina Litinovia. She tells him that she was recently reunited with Mishka, who died one week ago. When Katerina compliments the Count on his famous poem, he reveals that Mishka was the author of 'Where Is It Now?' As Mishka would have been arrested or killed for writing a revolutionary poem in the political climate of 1913, however, they decided to publish it under the Count's name.

Katerina gives the Count Mishka's great project: a handmade book titled *Bread and Salt*. The book is a compendium of quotations from famous literary works containing the word 'bread'. It concludes with the sentence Mishka was forced to cut from Chekov's letter.

BOOK FIVE

1954: Applause and Acclaim

Sofia is now a pianist with the Moscow Conservatory and is due to perform on tour in Paris in six months' time. Meanwhile, the Count secretly flips through the hotel's reservations book looking for bookings to suit his purpose. He settles on the 'combined dinner of the Presidium and the Council of Ministers': a meeting of the most powerful Soviet statesmen, which is due to take place on 11 June.

The Count is surprised to learn from Viktor Stepanovich that Sofia has withdrawn her name from the Conservatory Orchestra's tour. When he questions her about her it Sofia explains that she wants to stay at the hotel with him. The Count urges her to go bravely out into the world and assures her that, wherever in the world she plays, he will hear her.

Achilles Agonistes

Count Rostov has busied himself with preparations for Sofia's departure, hiring Viktor to help her rehearse, working on improving her French and taking a *Baedeker* travel guide for Paris from the lost property section in the basement. The next step in his plan is executed when he goes for his weekly appointment with Boris, the new barber. Boris is interrupted in his work by an urgent note from the manager summoning him to his office. Before the barber returns, announcing that he has been sent on a fool's mission, the Count plunders his glass cabinet, removing the bottle known as 'the Fountain of Youth' and a razor. Back in his room he uses the razor to cut out a map from the Baedeker and removes two hundred pages from the *Essays of Montaigne*.

Arrivederci

In early May, the Count lets himself into the room of an Italian couple and removes a shirt and pants from the man's wardrobe. He then visits the room of Pudgy Webster, an American vending machine salesman, and asks him to deliver a letter to a mutual acquaintance in Paris. After several drinks with the American, Count Rostov decides to return to the room of the Italian couple to steal a cap. All goes well until the Count is distracted by a brown paper package which contains matryoshka dolls. Failing to exit the room before the couple return, he is forced to hide in their closet. When his full bladder determines that he can hide no longer, the Count bursts from the closet, waking the couple as he leaves. Roughly translated, the resulting conversation (which takes place in Italian) is as follows:-

"What was that? Darling, wake up."

"What?"

"There is someone in the room!"

(Bump)

"Who's there?"

"Sorry."

"Claudio! Turn on the light!"

(Bam)

"Sorry"

(Crash)

"Goodbye!"

Adulthood

Sofia models the long gown the Marina has made for her Paris tour. The Count is speechless with admiration until he realises that the gown is backless.

At their regular meeting the Bishop asks how the arrangements for the important state dinner in June are going. When he learns that the Count is overseeing the function, the Bishop instructs Andrey to do it instead. The last minute change threatens to ruin the Count's plans.

An Announcement

The day before the state dinner Andrey announces that he is suffering from palsy – a condition which makes his hands shake. He tells the Bishop that, as he is in no fit state to serve men of importance, he has contacted the Kremlin to assure them that Headwaiter Rostov will oversee the dinner instead.

When the Count receives the guest list for the function and sees that there is no planned seating arrangement he realises that the attendees will find their natural positions at the table according to the political power they wield. The seats the men take will therefore speak volumes about who is to take Stalin's place as leader of the country.

During the state dinner, the Count hears every word that is said and notes that Premier Malenkov and General Secretary Khrushchev take the two centre seats at head of table. Towards the end of the evening it becomes clear that Krushchev has engineered the entire event when he asks the other diners to join him at the window. After his colleague gives a speech about the new nuclear power plant that has been built in Russia, Krushchev announces that, at 11 p.m., the plant will begin providing power to half of Moscow. The Count snuffs out the dinner candles, as instructed, and the attendees watch the lights of Moscow go out section by section and then reignite, even brighter than before.

Anecdotes

Just as Sofia is about to leave for Paris, the Count finally reveals his plan to her. Sofia is upset but reluctantly agrees to do as he asks. At the last minute she learns that the venue for the concert has been changed from the Palais Garnier to the Salle Pleyel. The Count retrieves a second travel guide to Paris from the basement and draws a new red line on its map. Before she goes to catch her train, she and the Count share a meal for two and he presents her with a photograph of himself.

An Association

The Count and Osip watch 'Casablanca' together. A big fan of Humphrey Bogart, Osip loves the scene where a petty thief, Ugarte, is caught by guards and implores Bogart's character, Rick, to help him. When Rick stands "impassively" as Ugarte is taken away and then urges his customers to continue enjoying themselves, Osip admires the "indifference" Bogart seems to express. Meanwhile, the Count imagines Sofia arriving in Paris chaperoned by Conservatory staff and members of the KGB.

Antagonists at Arms (And an Absolution)

For the next step in his plan the Count must steal a Scandinavian passport. With only 24 hours to go, a Finnish couple check into the hotel. The Count successfully slips into their room during the night, taking a passport and some Finnish currency. When he returns to his room, however, he finds the Bishop seated at the Grand Duke's desk waiting for him. Making sure that the Count has noted that he holds the first annotated Baedeker map of Paris, the Bishop leaves without a word.

Returning to his own office, the Bishop is shocked to find the Count sitting behind his desk holding two antique pistols. Using one of Sofia's favourite routes, the Count has dashed there before him and retrieved the dueling pistols from behind the secret panel.

At gunpoint, the Bishop reluctantly gives up his key to the office filing cabinets. Inside are files on Metropol guests and staff, listing their character flaws in detail. The Count's file is one of the thickest. In the early hours of the morning, when the hotel is quiet, the Count makes the Bishop carry the files to the basement and feed them into the furnace. He then takes a *Baedeker* on Finland from lost property and locks the Bishop in the storeroom with the silver service. Back on the landing, he sees the ghost of the one-eyed cat.

Apotheoses

The next day the Count packs a rucksack containing a few essentials, *Anna Karenina*, Mishka's project, and a bottle of Châteauneuf-du-Pape which he intends to drink in 1963 (ten years after his friend's death). After dinner he slips into the coatroom, taking a coat and hat belonging to Harrison Salisbury before making his way to the lobby.

In Paris, Sofia receives applause for her performance at the Salle Pleyel and then locks herself into a bathroom. She puts on the shirt and slacks stolen from the Italian guest, cuts her hair short with Helena's egret scissors and then dyes the distinctive white streak in her hair with the 'fountain of youth' (intended for covering grey in gentlemen's beards). Finally, she puts the cap on and slips out into the streets of Paris, following the red route on the map the Count gave to her.

At the American Embassy, Paris, Richard Vanderwhile is informed that a young man has arrived seeking asylum. The 'boy' turns out to be Sofia Rostov. Richard gives Sofia a parcel from the Count which contains gold coins hidden inside a butchered copy of Montaigne's essays. In return, Sofia gives Richard her knapsack. Sewn inside the lining is a diagram of the seating at the combined dinner, along with a summary of each guest's personality and a detailed account of the events of the evening. There is also a note explaining how Richard should confirm Sofia's safe arrival.

Back in the Metropol, at the stroke of midnight, every telephone on the first floor begins to ring. Unnoticed in the chaos that ensues, the Count puts on Salisbury's coat and hat and walks out of the hotel.

AFTERWORD

Afterwards ...

Viktor Stepanovich leaves his apartment just before midnight and meets Count Rostov in a café. As they talk, a fight breaks out between two fruit sellers and, after the traders are ejected from the premises, an accordion player strikes up a tune to restore harmony. The incident reminds the Count of Osip's favourite scene in 'Casablanca' and he shares Osip's interpretation of it with Viktor.

The next morning KGB officers arrive at the Metropol to question Headwaiter Alexander Rostov. Unable to find him, they also discover that the Hotel Manager hasn't reported for work. Meanwhile Emile and Andrey, who knew nothing of the Count's plans, are presented with envelopes by the mailroom clerk. Similar envelopes are also delivered to Marina, Audrius and Vasily. Inside each is a letter thanking the receiver for their friendship along with four gold coins. When Emile asks what is to become of him now that the Count has gone and Andrey is suffering from palsy, Andrey proves that his hands are as trustworthy as ever by juggling the gold coins.

Inside the Kremlin, the Chief Administrator of the Secret Police is informed that Sofia Rostov has gone missing in Paris, that Alexander Rostov is missing from the Metropol and that the Hotel Manager has been found locked in a storeroom. He also learns that the Count is assumed to have crossed the border into Finland, as a Finnish passport was stolen from the Metropol, as well as a travel guide for Finland. A man wearing a coat and hat stolen from the hotel has been seen boarding a train to Helsinki and the stolen garments were later found abandoned in a washroom at a Russian terminus. The Chief Administrator suppresses a smile on hearing the news. The scar above his ear reveals him to be none other than

Humphrey Bogart fan, Osip Glebnikov.

The narrator reveals that, after meeting Count Rostov in a café, Viktor Stepanovich boarded a train to Helsinki wearing Harrison Salisbury's stolen hat and coat and abandoned the clothes in a washroom before returning home. A year later Viktor watches 'Casablanca' for the first time. Observing the scene described by the Count carefully he notes that, as Rick resumes his duties, he sets right a cocktail glass that has been knocked over in the fight. Viktor interprets this gesture as faith that it is possible to "restore some sense of order in the world" through small but significant actions.

And Anon

Summer 1954. In Nizhny Novgorod Count Rostov returns to Idlehour only to find that it has been burned to the ground. He enters an inn and approaches a "willowy woman" sitting at the back.

HISTORICAL CONTEXT

The Russian Revolution

Before the Russian Revolution, the Russian Empire was ruled by a tsarist regime. Absolute monarchs in the old-fashioned sense, Russian tsars owned most of the land, commanded the army and even controlled the church, as their power was thought to be granted by divine right. Unsurprisingly, this system led to the abuse of power, perfectly illustrated by the reign of Tsar Nicholas II. Dissolving the Russian parliament whenever it crossed him, Nicholas did nothing to improve Russia's backward economy and maintained the centuries-long oppression of the lower classes, who earned little and often went hungry.

By 1917, dissatisfaction with the tsar's regime had come to a head, largely due to the country's ill-advised involvement in World War I. Russian troops were sent to fight without training or adequate equipment and, as a result, sustained massive losses. Two million Russian soldiers lost their lives, while food supplies and the Russian economy were further disrupted by the cost of involvement in the war. Led by Vladimir Lenin and revolutionaries known as the Bolsheviks, Russian peasants and members of the working classes openly revolted, demanding the abdication of Nicholas II, who was placed under house arrest with his family at Alexander Palace.

In 1918 Tsar Nicholas II and his family were executed, bringing Russia's history of imperial rule to a bloody end. The end of Russian imperialism was accompanied by the erasure of the Russian nobility and the elimination of organised religion in the country. As all classes of nobility were abolished and estates seized as state property, some aristocrats were killed while many others fled the country. Those who remained were deemed "former people" and were either killed in the Great Purge or survived by living anonymously. Meanwhile, atheism was promoted in schools and many Russian Orthodox churches were demolished or repurposed.

The Russian Civil War

Shortly after the Revolution, in 1918, the Russian Civil War commenced. During the war the Red Army (the Bolsheviks, revolutionaries and working classes) battled the Whites (anti-revolutionaries including the bourgeoisie, the aristocracy, army officers and Cossacks). The Bolsheviks' notorious campaign of torture, oppression and mass killings during this time became known as 'The Red Terror' and it was the forces of the Red Army who were eventually victorious.

Lenin and Stalin

With the removal of Tsar Nicholas II, the tsarist regime was replaced by the virtual dictatorship of the Bolshevik leader, Vladimir Lenin. His new Communist government moved the capital of Russia from Petrograd (now Saint Petersburg) to Moscow and in 1922 the Russian Empire became the Soviet Union. When Lenin died in 1924 he was replaced by another prominent Bolshevik, Joseph Stalin.

Stalin (nicknamed Soso) was the leader of the Soviet Union until his death in 1953. During his leadership the country underwent great change which included the shift from a rural to an industrial economy, the censorship of religious worship and artistic expression and the promotion of equal opportunities for women. While this period of Russian history saw the country emerge as a power to be reckoned with, Stalin's methods of achieving this success were, at best, controversial. Both the KGB and the Iron Curtain were established during Stalin's rule and the Soviet Union became the second country in the world to develop a nuclear weapon. The period also saw an escalation of hostility with the Western World (the Cold War).

Stalin's ruthless determination to make the Soviet Union a world power was demonstrated in his five-year-plan, put into practice from 1928 to 1932. The aim of the plan was to transform Russia's rural economy into an industrial one while, at the same time, maximising the country's agricultural output. Previously isolated areas were turned into massive industrial centres producing coal, oil, steel and electricity. Meanwhile, in the countryside, farms owned by kulaks (a class of relatively affluent farming peasants) were seized and became part of a collective farming system employing hundreds of peasants. Many kulaks slaughtered their own livestock rather than give them up to this huge farming operation. Many of those who resisted the takeover of their land were killed or deported to labour camps. Once established, collective farming proved a failure. The enforced changes disrupted the food supply and led to large-scale famines which reached their peak in 1933. As a result, more that 30 million Russian citizens died of starvation.

To meet the five-year-plan's ambitious goals, prisoners were used as an additional source of labour. As pressure grew to meet Stalin's unrealistic targets, there was a corresponding increase in the prisoner population, as people were sentenced to forced labour for minor offences or on trumped-up charges. Thousands of workers died as a result of their harsh working conditions and those who received wages for their labour were paid badly. Housing conditions were crowded and unsanitary and ordinary citizens did not have access to consumer goods.

Another infamous characteristic of Stalin's government was the Great Purge of the 1930s. In an attempt to remove anyone who might oppose him, Stalin ordered the arrest of millions of people, most of whom were innocent. Many Communist Party members, government bureaucrats and officers of the Red Army were accused of political crimes ranging from espionage to conspiracies to overthrow the government. Punishment came in the form of execution or exile to the notorious Gulag labour camps in Siberia. Here prisoners were forced to work in the harshest of conditions and with pitifully inadequate equipment, mining copper or coal by hand, excavating frozen ground with pickaxes and felling trees with handsaws. An estimated 13 million people are estimated to have died in the Great Purge, either from execution or as a result of being worked to death in the labour camps.

As well as keeping tight control over potential political dissidents, Stalin heavily influenced the artistic output of the country through the Ministry of Culture, formed in 1936. The Ministry's role was to ensure that Soviet film, music, art and literature did nothing to 'sabotage' the aims and ideologies of the Communist Party. Seeking to minimise the influence of Western culture, the Ministry also censored artistic works that might be viewed as critical of the Soviet Union. Social realism emerged as the government-approved artistic style, while other forms of expression were repressed. As a result, certain books and the work of some composers were banned and many writers were either killed or imprisoned. While emigration restrictions legally prevented Soviet citizens from leaving the country, artistic performers often took advantage of international tours to escape the country's oppressive regime. A number of ballet dancers defected during world tours, while figure skaters, gymnasts and several football players escaped during the Olympics and the European Cup respectively.

Nikita Khrushchev

When Stalin died in 1953, a struggle for power began between prominent members of the Communist Party. After several years of wrangling amongst a collective leadership, Nikita Khrushchev emerged as the leader of the Soviet Union in 1958. Once Stalin was safely out of the way, Khrushchev denounced many of the former leader's policies and introduced a process of de-Stalinization, revising many of the laws introduced by the former leader, bringing an end to forced labour and improving conditions for prisoners in the Gulag camps. He also re-named many places or buildings named after Stalin. Unfortunately, Khrushchev's belief that nuclear weapons were the best form of national defence led to tensions with the West, resulting in the Cuban Missile Crisis. He was deposed by Leonid Brezhnev in 1964.

The Hotel Metropol

Built in 1905, the Metropol quickly established itself as Russia's grand hotel, comparable to New York's Plaza or Claridge's in London. Priding itself on luxury and impeccable service, the Metropol was the first hotel in Moscow to boast telephones in the rooms and hot water. Over the years, the hotel attracted the rich and famous, with John Steinbeck, e.e. cummings and Lillian Hellman all writing accounts of their stays there.

The changing face of the Hotel Metropol during the twentieth century offers an excellent insight into the turbulent changes taking place in the country at the time. Damaged during the Russian Revolution, the hotel was then restored but not immediately for its former purpose. After switching the Soviet Union's capital city from St. Petersburg to Moscow, Lenin required a temporary building to house his new government. Renaming the Metropol 'the Second House of the Soviets', the Communist Party seized the hotel, ejected the guests and set up government departments in its rooms.

By the 1920s, as the Soviet Union began to open up relationships with other European countries, Communist leaders realised that the hotels in Moscow were important in helping to form visitors' first impressions of the country. Eager to present the new Russia as progressive and flourishing to the outside world, the state ensured that its flagship hotel was restored to something like its former grandeur. The Metropol, therefore, became an oasis of luxury and pleasure within an austere and repressive state.

The Metropol remains a grand hotel today. Photographs of the building as it is now can be viewed at www.metropol-moscow.ru

History in *A Gentleman in Moscow*

Given the period in which it is set *A Gentleman in Moscow* may, at first, seem light on historical context. While Count Rostov's house arrest illustrates one of the consequences of the Russian Revolution (the abolition of the aristocracy) the protagonist's situation effectively places him outside of history. An apparently timeless oasis, the Metropol seems to offer an escape from the drastic and often brutal changes taking place in the rest of the country. Read more closely, however, and a different picture emerges. Over the years, the Metropol is subtly changed by outside forces, while the Count vicariously experiences historical events through his encounters with the guests who come and go. To provide a fuller picture, asides from the third-person narrator instruct the reader on major events that take place beyond the scope of the story.

While there are much worse places to be than the Metropol after the Russian Revolution, the Count still observes signs of austerity that reflect the mood and economics of the outside world. These tell-tale signs can be found everywhere, from the lack of

Christmas decorations in the Piazza to the banning of the wine list in the Boyarsky; from the closed-up florist in the lobby to the alchemy Emile is forced to work in the kitchen, transforming cheap ingredients into delicious dishes. Luxury and frivolity have all but been removed from the hotel, as the ballroom is utilised as a venue for Bolshevik Assemblies and government bureaucrats type directives on the second floor.

More changes emerge, however, as the post-revolutionary government begins to concern itself with Russia is viewed by the rest of the world. For the benefit of foreign visitors, Christmas decorations reappear, jazz is played in the bar and the Russian women who enter the hotel have discarded their peasant clothing for chic, colourful fashions. While these changes are welcome, the author makes it clear that they are publicity-driven and have nothing to with boosting the morale of the average Russian citizen. While select members of the Communist Party begin to enjoy state dinners in the hotel's function rooms, the majority of Russians are still going without the basics.

Amor Towles also cleverly reflects the increasingly tense political atmosphere of the country through the hotel's changing staff. The replacement of the lazy but innocuous manager, Halecki, with the sinister Bishop tells us a great deal about Stalin's regime. While the Bishop's promotion is a clear case of nepotism within the Communist Party, his petty bureaucracy and the files he keeps on his guests and staff perfectly reflect Stalin's repressive style of government.

While changes at the hotel provide a rough guide to the political climate outside the Metropol, the Count's interactions with other people provide more specific examples of how the country is changing. His monthly meetings with Osip demonstrate the way the Soviet Communist Party has transformed from a revolutionary force to a shrewdly political engine. Formerly Captain of the Red Army, Osip learns what he can from the Count about other nations, understanding the importance of knowing the enemy. Thanks to this ability to adapt to the new political climate, Osip becomes Chief Administrator of Security. The Count also rubs shoulders with a number of important historical figures when he waits upon the combined state dinner. While the dinner, with its theatrical demonstration of nuclear power, is fictional it effectively illustrates the process by which Nikita Khrushchev emerged as the new Soviet leader.

Perhaps most historically significant, however, are the fates of the Count's closest friends. Anna's acting career is shown to be at the mercy of changes in political ideology and is saved only by her close association with the Minister of Culture. Meanwhile, Nina and Mishka both fall foul of the new Communist government which they initially have faith in.

At the beginning of the novel, while the Count's life is effectively erased by the Russian Revolution, Nina and Mishka are excited at the progress and equality they believe the new era will bring. Nina joins a youth division of the Communist Party to help implement Stalin's five-year-plan, earnest in the belief that collective farming is a "historical necessity". Mishka looks forward to a new era of revolutionary poetry exemplified by the work of the 'poet laureate of the Revolution', Vladimir Mayakovsky. The process by which both characters are disillusioned highlights the grim reality of 1930s Russia. By volunteering to help with the collectivization of agriculture, Nina comes to realise that the process involves the destruction of the lives of those who previously farmed it. She is also witness to the widespread famine which was to kill over 30 million Russians. In Mishka's case, his disillusionment is with the artistic censorship imposed by the state, illustrated when he is forced to remove a sentence praising the bread in Berlin from one of Chekov's letters. His hopes of a new era of revolutionary poetry are dashed as one-by-one, the poets he admires are silenced by the state until his literary hero, Vladimir Mayakovsky, dies after apparently having shot himself in the heart. Both characters learn the consequences of opposing the government when Mishka is sentenced to hard labour in Siberia, while it can only be assumed that Nina and her husband join the millions of others who simply disappeared during Stalin's Great Purge.

Where historical events cannot be adequately conveyed through the experiences of the characters, the novel's third-person narrator fills the reader in with brief but telling asides. As Nina hops on a train, full of enthusiasm about her mission, the narrator explains why she will become disillusioned with the five-year-plan, detailing the forced exile of the kulaks from their land, the disruption that would take place in agricultural output and the resulting famine that would kill millions of Ukrainian peasants. Similarly, when

Mishka returns to Moscow in 1946 after his exile to Siberia, the narrator elaborates on the historical events that have etched themselves upon the streets. The decommissioned tanks that stand in front of the Kremlin prompt a description of World War II and the failure of invading German troops to reach Moscow. Meanwhile, the queues of people visiting Lenin's tomb prompt a brief description of the transition to Stalinist Russia. With these discrete brushstrokes Amor Towles provides a surprisingly wide-ranging overview of Russian history without being obtrusive or heavy-handed in the detail.

STYLE

The Narrator

Although Count Rostov is the protagonist of *A Gentleman in Moscow,* his story is told by an omniscient third-person narrator. Witty and elegant in tone, the narrator's voice has much in common with that of the Count. Towles' choice of a third-person narrator for his novel is a masterly touch. While a first-person account from the charming Count himself might seem the obvious way to go, the more detached narrator injects the novel with greater flexibility and scope.

A Gentleman in Moscow is very much the story of Count Rostov. Nevertheless, the author's use of a third-person narrator allows the reader to dip in and out of other viewpoints in the novel. After the Count's first liaison with Anna, for example, we are treated to Anna's perspective as she fumes for weeks over the impertinent way the Count hung up her blouse before leaving her room. Another short chapter (Addendum of Book Four) describes a day in the life of Andrey, revealing that the unfailingly cheerful maître d' lost his only son in the Battle of Berlin. These switches of viewpoint not only give the reader more insight into the other characters but also allow the narrative to briefly leave the confines of the Hotel Metropol. Wry footnotes add to this effect, providing historical background and information about the plight of the Russian people.

The narrator's God-like viewpoint also occasionally allows for the foretelling of future events. When Count Rostov opens Nina's Christmas gift, for example, the narrator undercuts the cosy mood he has created by informing the reader that, in four years' time, Rostov will be preparing to throw himself off the roof of the Metropol. Meanwhile, in a footnote the narrator offers a tip-off to readers, urging them to take note of a seemingly inconsequential character (Anna's balding, round-faced suitor) as he will prove to be important to the plot.

This narrative playfulness is also brilliantly illustrated in the narrator's lengthy footnote about Russian literature. In arguing that Russian literature can be difficult for readers to follow, he blames authors for using different names for the same character, drawing upon a limited range of standard Russian names (Anna, Andrey and Alexander) and for introducing characters who prove superfluous to the story. Having already committed the first two sins in his own narrative, the narrator then tells a long story about Prince Nikolai Petrov who, he assures us, we do not need to remember, as he will not appear in the novel again. Constantly engaging with the reader, the narrator assumes that his audience has the wit required to follow his digressions and appreciate his ironies. Instead of spelling everything out, certain connections are left for readers to work out for themselves. When a new assistant manager is hired at the Metropol, for example, we are not told directly that it is the Bishop but left to make the realisation when we learn that the manager wears "the smile of an ecclesiast." Similarly, when the Chief Administrator of the Kremlin receives news of the Count's escape, only the distinctive scar on his head reveals to the reader that this is Osip. Such details announce that this is a clever narrative and readers will need to keep their wits about them if they are going to keep up.

Tone

A Gentleman in Moscow makes many references to Russian literature but the novel's light and frothy tone has more in common with P.G. Wodehouse than Tolstoy or Dostoevsky. Social realism flies out of the window as antique pistols are found behind secret panels, wild geese are chased down hotel corridors and the characters step in and out of wardrobes more frequently than the cast of a bedroom farce. Up until its fifth and final section, when an urgent sense of narrative drive takes over and all the loose strands are drawn together, the novel is a collage of witty conversations, amusing encounters and improbable antics. Despite its levity, however, *A Gentleman in Moscow* is undoubtedly a work of literary historical fiction, demonstrating that a novel can be rich, clever and many-layered and still remain uplifting.

Structure

While much of the novel describes a collection of seemingly random incidents, its meticulously organised plot and structure is far from chaotic. Everything in *A Gentleman in Moscow* falls into a carefully prescribed pattern, from the chapter titles, which all begin with the letter 'a' to the deliberately rigid time structure of the plot. Astute readers may have noticed that the dates in the novel follow a numerical sequence. Beginning on 21 June 1922, the chapters proceed on a doubling principle, moving forward by one day, then two days; five days then 10 days; three weeks then six weeks, etc. until by halfway through the novel, sixteen years have passed. In the second half of the novel this pattern is reversed and the timescale works on a halving principle, moving forward eight years, then four, then two, etc. until the day the Count walks out of the Hotel Metropol.

Even the accumulation of apparently random details in the first half of the novel is shown to have its purpose in the second. The moustache-snipping incident with the angry man in the barber's leads to the Count's friendship with Nina which, later, leads to his adoption of Sofia. Count Rostov's decision to contradict a poor wine recommendation made by the Bishop leads to the removal of the hotel's wine list and provokes the unwavering hostility of the future hotel manager. Sofia's humorous game of racing through the hotel to lie in wait for the Count leads to an accident but also proves useful when the Count uses her secret route to reach the Bishop's office before him. The dueling pistols he holds when the Bishop arrives are, of course, the very same ones he described to Nina in a story years before.

Just as no encounter is shown to be meaningless, many objects occur and recur, taking on greater significance as the novel progresses. After the Count gives up on reading the *Essays of Montaigne* the weighty volume takes on greater usefulness as a hiding place for gold coins. Helena's egret scissors come in useful when Sofia cuts her hair with them, disguising herself as a boy (as does the 'Fountain of Youth' – the hair dye first cryptically referred to during the Count's trip to the barbers at the beginning of the novel). Meanwhile, the silver summoner, discovered by the Count and Nina on one of their first adventures, connects mother and daughter when Sofia uses it during her last meal with Count

Rostov. In this way, the author weaves an intricate web of meaning between incidents and objects, suggesting nothing is ever trivial or insignificant.

LOCATION

The Hotel Metropol

The very nature of the Count's predicament means that locations for the novel are limited. As he is placed under house arrest in the Hotel Metropol, Moscow, almost all of the action takes place in this grand Art Nouveau hotel. While it hardly seems a severe punishment to be forced to stay in these luxurious surroundings, the Count immediately suffers a drastic lifestyle change when he is turfed out of the opulence of Suite 317 with its large windows overlooking Theatre Square to a cramped attic space with a tiny window. His new accommodation perfectly epitomises the Count's transition from nobleman to 'former person'. Situated on the sixth floor and reached by a utility stair, the space was once the servants' quarters before being repurposed as a junk room.

Throughout the novel certain room numbers take on particular significance and the Count is not the only character whose change of room reflects a change of fortune. When Anna first seduces the Count she is at the height of her desirability and fame. This status is reflected in her occupation of Suite 208 – a grand room decorated in the style of a Venetian palazzo. By 1928, however, as her movie career takes a downturn, she has to make do with room 428 which overlooks the trolley tracks (and is incidentally the room the Count steals an Italian gentleman's clothes from later in the novel).

Surprisingly, downsizing rooms turns out to have its compensations for the Count. Before his removal to the attic room, he is only familiar with the parts of the hotel designed for the eyes of the guests. His move to the servants' quarters, however, marks the start of his exploration of the hidden parts of the hotel. With the help of Nina and her passkey, the Count discovers a labyrinth of secret places ranging from the very bottom to the top of the hotel: linen closets; pantries; the coatroom; the switchboard;

43

an electric room, the basement and even the roof. In exploring these out-of-bounds areas he discovers the hotel contains wonders he never dreamed of, such as the silver summoner in the pantry and the bee hives on the roof. Exploring the hotel's secret spaces also opens the Count's mind to the idea that it may be possible to expand the tiny space he has been allocated. Realising that the back of his wardrobe has been built into an old doorframe, he breaks through to the closet of the room next door. Claiming this second room as his own, the Count furnishes it as a study and feels that the secret nature of the space makes it all the more capacious.

During the Count's enforced stay in the hotel some of the most turbulent periods in Russian history are taking place. Throughout it all, the hotel endures as a nostalgic oasis. Even this grand hotel, however, does not remain untouched by historical change. At the beginning of the novel a sense of utilitarianism has pervaded the hotel's corridors. The Communist bureaucrats still resident and typing directives on the second floor are the legacy of the hotel's recent history as a temporary seat for Lenin's new government. Meanwhile, any sense of frivolity has been erased from the ballroom – now a meeting place for Bolshevik Assemblies. This mood of austerity also extends to the lobby where the once flourishing florist has closed down and to the restaurant kitchen, where the chef if forced to perform miracles with cabbage and cornmeal for the few diners who drift through its doors. By 1924, however, changes in government policy are reflected in the hotel's atmosphere. Keen to promote trade relations with other countries, the Communist Party ensure that glamour is reinjected into the hotel to make a good impression on foreign visitors. The hotel's restaurants, the Boyarsky and the Piazza, once again become bustling hubs of life, while jazz is played in the Shalyapin, the American-style bar, as foreign diplomats mix with ballet dancers from the Bolshoi. Even the Communist Party's use of the hotel is shown to become somewhat more decadent, as Bolshevik Assemblies are replaced by dinners of state.

Idlehour

Idlehour is the evocative name of the Rostov estate in Nizhny Novgorod where the Count grew up. The location of many nostalgic memories, particularly of his grandmother and beloved sister, Idlehour represents home for the Count, even though he was forced to abandon it in 1918 after the execution of Tsar Nicholas II. The limited possessions he can fit into his attic room are all reminders of the great estate that he left behind. They also serve to emphasise the dramatic contrast between the Count's life before and after the Russian Revolution.

In the final pages of the novel the Count returns to Idlehour. While the apple trees he fondly remembers from childhood are still there (although slightly ragged) he finds that Idlehour itself has been burned to the ground, leaving only the chimneys behind. The Count's serene smile, however, indicates that he accepts the inevitability of change.

THEMES & IMAGERY

THEMES

Nobility & Class

When the Count is placed under house arrest and forced to move to more humble quarters, he also loses his status as a nobleman. This loss of aristocratic clout is underlined when members of the hotel staff are no longer permitted to address him as "Your Excellency". As the title of the novel emphasises, however, while Count Rostov may lose his title, he remains, at all times, a gentleman. What identifies him as such is not his aristocratic background but his courtesy, impeccable manners and respect for others, no matter what their social standing might be.

These characteristics are clearly illustrated when the Count is visited in his new cramped quarters by hotel staff members Andrey, Vasily and Marina and he invites them in to celebrate. The Count treats his guests with the same courtesy he would demonstrate if hosting a party for fellow aristocrats at Idlehour. When a young Nina interrogates him on the "rules of being a princess", the Count emphasises the importance of combining good manners with respect for people of all ages and classes when he relates the story of Princess Golitsyn who forgets the grand party she is about to attend in order to help and take tea with 'the crone of Kudrovo'.

It could be argued that Amor Towles is in danger of glamorising the Russian aristocracy in his novel, brushing aside the part many of the nobility played in the oppression of the country's peasant classes. Towles goes to some lengths, however, to clarify that the Count has not been corrupted by his privilege. When he recalls helping the caretaker of Idlehour repair fencing as a boy, the memory emphasises both his innate lack of class prejudice and the pleasure he takes in hard work, separating him from the exploitative idle rich.

The Passage of Time

The time structure of *A Gentleman in Moscow* is a particularly unusual feature of the novel. Working on a doubling time principle in the first half of the novel and a halving principle in the second, the structure reflects both the pace of the plot and the way the Count experiences the passage of time. Beginning with intervals of only days between chapters, the first half of the novel progresses to intervals of several years. This suggests not only a lack of significant incidents in these periods as the Count spends longer and longer in the hotel but also that, as he gets older, the Count feels as if entire years have passed in a blur. In the second half of the novel, however, time begins to accelerate leading up to Sofia's departure for Paris. Aware of the tight deadline leading up to Sofia's planned defection and the things that must be accomplished to make it run smoothly, the Count begins to think of time in terms of months, days and hours left. His previous "life of the purposefully unrushed" becomes a race against time.

The importance of time in the novel is emphasised by Count Rostov's twice-tolling clock. The Count's father had this unique timepiece commissioned to underline his own theories about how each day should ideally be spent. While, by the first chime at noon, a full day's work should have been accomplished, by the second chime, at midnight, everyone in the household should be asleep in bed. Ironically, as the Count's life becomes entangled with those of others he finds himself hearing the clock strike midnight increasingly often. He sits up until midnight to open his Christmas gift from Nina; he plans to kill himself at midnight; Sofia hugs him for the first time before getting into bed as the clock strikes midnight and, once she is a woman, he hears the clock's second chime as he waits impatiently for her to return from her musical debut. The message seems to be that, despite his father's theory, a full life cannot always be crammed into a prescribed set of hours.

The passing of time is, of course, a reminder of our mortality. This is emphasised by the Rostov family tradition of celebrating the ten year anniversaries of loved ones' deaths. It is also illustrated in the moment when the Count visits Suite 317, finds the family clock has stopped, and sets it going again. As the Count observes the effects of the ageing process on Emile and Andrey, the reader notes these same effects upon the Count. Aware that he no longer experiences life with the same intensity as in his youth, he feels his role is now to encourage his adopted daughter to live life to the full. This notion of the cyclical nature of life and time itself is also illustrated earlier in the novel when the Count draws parallels between the grand balls that once took place in the ballroom and the Bolshevik Assemblies that have replaced them. The similarity he sees between the behaviour of aristocratic socialites and scruffy Bolsheviks demonstrates that while time eventually moves on without us, human nature remains essentially the same.

Progress & Destruction

As his time under house arrest mounts up, the Count increasingly feels that the world is moving on without him. Outside the hotel, streets that he once knew well change their names. Inside, staff members leave and are replaced by inexperienced substitutes, Nina grows up and eventually moves to a large apartment for Party officials with her father, and even Abram's bees abandon their hives. The Count's sense that progress is erasing his identity is part of a wider exploration of the connection between progress and destruction in the novel.

One of the main aims of the new Soviet government is to transform the country into a major world power through progress. While this aim is achieved, the novel demonstrates what a ruthless process progress turns out to be. Although the Count is mistrustful of progress from the start, Mishka and Nina are initially excited at the prospect. Nina views Stalin's five-year- plan as a "historical necessity" and Mishka looks forward to the end of the oppression of the people and the emergence of a new revolutionary poetry. Neither character, however, is prepared for the means by which this progress will be achieved. Through first-hand experience Nina comes to realise that the introduction of collectivized farming involves the forced exile of the resident farmers and a famine that kills millions. Mishka's dreams of an end to oppression and a new era of free artistic expression are similarly shattered as writers are silenced and even driven to suicide by the heavy-handed censorship of the Communist government.

When Mishka returns from Siberia to Moscow in 1946 he notes the empty space where Kazan Cathedral used to be. Having stood in Red Square for three hundred years, the cathedral was razed to the ground by the Bolsheviks in 1936. This was partly to make room for military parades and partly a symbolic gesture to underline the death of Christianity in the Soviet state. Mishka bitterly proclaims to the Count that he has realised one of the defining characteristics of the Russian people is their unsentimental ability to destroy the things they have created. To make his point he lists many other examples – the moment in 1812 when the citizens of Moscow set fire to the city rather than permit Napoleon to claim it; the decision of many peasants to kill their livestock rather than give them up to collectivized farming; the erection and then removal of statues of the country's heroes and the silencing of great poets. This ruthlessly destructive Russian streak also seems to be corroborated by an incident the Count witnessed in 1918. Having always admired the sound of the great bells from the Church of the Ascension, he was dismayed to see them being flung unceremoniously from the bell tower, ready for repurposing as artillery. When an abbot from the monastery remonstrated, he too was thrown from the bell tower.

While the Count and Mishka are disturbed by the Russian willingness to destroy in the pursuit of progress, Osip believes that it is one of the country's great strengths. This is expressed in his admiration of Humphrey Bogart's portrayal of unsentimental ruthlessness in the film 'Casablanca'. Osip sees this ability to sweep aside the past as a trait shared by the Soviet Union and the USA and believes it is the key to becoming a world power. In the end, however, it is Richard Vanderwhile who offers a more balanced viewpoint, suggesting that "grand things persist", even in the face of progress and destruction. This idea is echoed in Mishka's reaction to Moscow after years of absence for, while he fixates on the destruction of Kazan Cathedral in Red Square, he also cannot help marvelling at how many of the "old facades" in Theatre Square remain standing.

The notion of destruction and rejuvenation as a natural and eternal cycle is also emphasised in the Count's reflection on the bells from the Church of the Ascension. While he mourns their transformation into artillery, he is also aware that the bells were originally made from Napoleon's cannons, which in turn had been made from the bells at La Rochelle and, one day, may well become bells again is some other location. This theory is underlined by the eventual real-life fate of Kazan Cathedral which was painstakingly reconstructed when the Communist regime came to an end.

Home & Exile

When sentenced to house arrest, the Count reflects that he is hardly the first to suffer this fate. Exile has been used as a punishment from the dawn of mankind when God first banished Adam from Eden. He notes, however, that the Russians are the first race to have the idea "of sending a man into exile at home." This tradition began in the 18th century when tsars began exiling their enemies to Siberia instead of throwing them out of the country altogether. The fiendish punishment proved particularly hard to bear for it prevented the 'criminal' from starting a completely new life, while leaving them to dwell on the elements of Russian life that are lost to them.

Both Mishka and Nina's husband are exiled to less hospitable regions of the Soviet Union for 'crimes' against the state. The tension between remaining at home whilst being in a state of exile is most ironically reflected, however, in the Count's situation. While he is permitted to remain resident at Moscow's finest hotel, he is denied many of the pleasures that previously accompanied that experience. Stripped of his spacious suite, his view of Theatre Square and his pleasurable jaunts around the city, the Count remains in Moscow but is forced to stand completely outside of its life. As time goes on this state of exile leaves the Count utterly purposeless, leading to his decision to end his own life. Significantly, however, it is at this moment that Abram's bees return to the hotel, producing honey from the apple blossom in Nizhny Novgorod. This nostalgic reminder of his original home is enough to give Count Rostov the motivation to live.

At the end of the novel, when the Count escapes the hotel, he does not flee the country but returns to Nizhny Novgorod. When he finds that his childhood home is now nothing but a ruin, however, he remains surprisingly unperturbed. This reflects his realisation that while places inevitably change over time, our memories of home remain an unassailable constant.

Property

When the Count is exiled from Suite 317 to an attic room, he is told that he can keep only those possessions that will fit in the small space. The rest of his belongings will become "the property of the People." This illustrates the hypocrisy of members of the Soviet Communist Party who condemned the possession of expensive luxuries by the aristocracy and then confiscated them for their own use. By attaching numbered copper plates to these items, identifying them as the property of the People, they salved their consciences while enjoying the rewards.

The possessions that Count Rostov chooses to keep illustrate that, for him, the value of an object lies in its associations. Every item he selects has associations with a loved one – from his sister's egret-shaped scissors to his grandmother's opera glasses and his godfather's desk. By the end of the novel, as the Count escapes the hotel, his rucksack contains only the bare essentials along with his copy of *Anna Karenina*, Mishka's project and a bottle of Châteauneuf-du-Pape.

Purpose

The poem 'Where Is It Now?' which opens the novel is a rumination on how to find purpose in the face of change. This is a subject which becomes particularly pertinent to Count Rostov (the supposed author of the poem).

When the Count faces the Bolshevik committee at the beginning of the novel, one of its members expresses surprise that the author of 'Where Is It Now?' has become "a man so obviously without purpose." These words prove to be unfortunately prophetic for, while the Count tries to make the best of his circumstances, he feels increasingly superfluous as the world moves on without him. Stripped of his title and his former routines, the Bolsheviks' definition of him as a 'former person' feels horribly accurate.

This crisis over his lack of purpose culminates in the Count's decision to take his own life. His suicide attempt is interrupted, however, by Abram's excited announcement that, after a long absence, his bees have returned to their rooftop hives. When the Count discovers that the bees have made a two-hundred-mile round trip to feed on the apple tree nectar in Nizhny Novgorod, his own sense of purpose is reawakened. From this moment he makes it his mission to find new purpose in his life. Taking a job as headwaiter in the Boyarsky restaurant, the Count puts his knowledge of fine wine and food and his instinct for seating arrangements to good use. Rather than feeling demeaned by his transition from aristocratic diner to a member of staff, the Count takes real satisfaction in performing his role to the very best of his abilities. When Viktor watches the scene in 'Casablanca' where Humphrey Bogart adjusts a cocktail glass after a fracas, he is immediately reminded of the Count and his purposeful attitude towards work. By paying attention to such small details, he somehow restores "some sense of order in the world".

Count Rostov is one of a number of dedicated members of staff who ensure the smooth-running of the grand hotel. Each of these individuals, while performing relatively mundane duties, demonstrates great pride in their work. The hotel barber, Yaroslav, is a maestro of the scissors, cutting hair with an unrivalled elegance and speed. Emile, the chef of the Boyarsky, only truly comes alive when he enters his kitchen and can turn the meanest ingredients into culinary gold. Meanwhile Andrey, the maître d', anticipates the every need of his diners "as his hands fulfilled their purpose at every turn." Only the inept and supercilious Bishop strikes a discordant note in what is otherwise a finely-tuned symphony of industry and purpose.

The Count is not the only character forced to find new purpose in a changing world. Viktor Stepanovich is a trained musician who finds the only way of profitably using his talents is as the conductor of the Piazza band. Similarly, the talented artist the Count observes sketching in the Piazza turns out to be a former architect, now using his skills to produce illustrations for a brochure of the city's finest hotels. While the new Communist regime has no use for innovative architectural design, it does require flattering pictures of its attractions to entice foreign visitors. This ability to adapt is the theme of one of the Count's favourite stories: the moths of Manchester. An example of rapid evolution, these nineteenth century moths transformed from white to black to camouflage themselves in an increasingly polluted industrial city. Count Rostov is particularly fond of this story as the moths embody the ability to not only survive but flourish in a rapidly changing world – a characteristic that becomes highly desirable in post-revolutionary Russia.

Literature

A Gentleman in Moscow is a book for book lovers. Almost an entire guide could be dedicated to the wide-ranging literary references in the novel, from the Count's comparison of his imprisonment to that of Edmond Dantès in *The Count of Monte Cristo* to a nod to the children's classic *The Lion, the Witch and the Wardrobe* when he discovers a secret world in the back of his closet.

One of the Count's many refined characteristics is his love of literature. Ironically, however, while house arrest gives him all the time in the world to read, the reading material available to him is sadly limited. With all his favourite books (by Dickens, Balzac and Tolstoy) still in Paris, the Count has to make do with the rather dry library he has inherited from his father. After a valiant attempt to plough through *The Essays of Montaigne*, he gives up and returns to an old favourite – Tolstoy's *Anna Karenina*. The Count's literary preferences reflect his personality, favouring the drama and emotion of Tolstoy's tragic romance over Montaigne's philosophical reasoning.

Anna Karenina is one of many Russian literary classics referenced in the novel. A great fan of Russian literature himself, Amor Towles keeps up a constant dialogue between his own modern Russian novel and the Russian greats. At first glance, *A Gentleman in Moscow* seems to have little in common with Russian epics such as Dostoevsky's *Crime and Punishment* or Tolstoy's *War and Peace* – novels not known for their optimistic mood or light-hearted tone. On closer examination, however, Towles' novel has more in common with the Russian epic than at first meets the eye. As well as the tendency to call one character by a confusing array of different names (playfully referred to in a footnote), Towles' use of an omniscient third-person narrator is typical of the nineteenth century Russian novel. Omniscient narrators were particularly popular with Russian authors as they could provide insight into the minds of the main characters without being limited to their perspectives. This means the narrator is also free to reflect on the wider historical context of the time, describing events which are outside the realm of the characters' experiences. Like *Anna Karenina,* Towles' novel focuses on the interior life of someone who is imprisoned. While the Count is unable to leave the Hotel Metropol, Anna feels trapped in an unhappy marriage. While for

Tolstoy, however, Anna's only possible trajectory is self-destruction, Towles' updated version of the Russian novel places a more positive spin on events, allowing the Count to progress beyond suicidal intentions to find fulfilment.

While Towles celebrates Russia's great literary heritage in his novel, he also highlights the crimes the Communist government committed against it. Forced to publish his poem 'Where Is It Now?' under the Count's name during the tsarist regime, Mishka anticipates that the new Communist government will nurture a new revolutionary literature. His expectations prove sadly misguided, however, as even those writers who supported the revolution become the target of censorship in post-revolutionary Russia. The incident where Mishka is forced to remove an enthusiastic description of German bread from one of Chekov's letters is an example of the petty and heavy-handed form the restrictions upon artistic expression took. Likewise, the suicide of the poet Vladimir Mayakovsy becomes a powerful symbol of the way the government killed their literary talent (both figuratively and literally).

Parenting

When Nina first approaches Count Rostov to ask after the whereabouts of his moustaches, he finds the intrusion unwelcome but is too polite to show it. Having had little experience of children, Nina's frank interrogation is something of a shock for a man accustomed to sophisticated adult conversation. As the Count's acquaintance with Nina grows, however, he comes to appreciate that the company of children has much to recommend it, from the fun they introduce to the way they refresh the perspective of jaded adults.

Nevertheless, when Nina asks the Count to take care of Sofia for her, he still feels utterly unequipped for the parental role. Usually supremely in control of his life, he finds himself completely out of his depth. Time drags as his attempts to amuse Sofia fall flat and he is embarrassed when Andrey has to discretely point out that small child need their food cutting up for them, as well as regular trips to the bathroom. His routine is also hopelessly disrupted as he struggles and fails to juggle work commitments, social engagements and romantic liaisons with childcare.

As time goes on, however, and the bond between the Count

and Sofia grows he realises that the child's arrival in his life has saved him from becoming stuck in a rut. He undergoes an important transition from living for his own pleasures to living for another. The Count not only accepts his weighty parental responsibilities but embraces them. This change of attitude is poignantly reflected in the conversation he has with Anna about 'conveniences'. While Anna declares that she would gladly emigrate to America for the "conveniences", the Count reflects that, "in the end, it has been the inconveniences that have mattered to me most."

Over the years the Count's relationship with Sofia highlights both the joys and anxieties of parenthood. These are illustrated from his pride in Sofia's intelligence and musical talent to his fury when he believes Viktor is seducing her, and his outrage at her "dressless dress". The Count's decision to break the terms of his house arrest in order to rush Sofia to hospital is made without the slightest hesitation and is a moving testament to the strength of his paternal love – as is his terror when he believes she may be left brain-damaged. His biggest parental challenge, however, comes when he realises that Sofia is about to withdraw from the Conservatory's tour of Paris in order to remain at the Metropol with him. Realising that he is in danger of trapping his daughter in the insular world of the hotel, he not only encourages her to go but begins to plan her defection, knowing that this means he will probably never see her again. This generous act of letting go is the ultimate expression of parental love.

Friendship

During his time under house arrest the Count finds joy and sustenance in his friendships with others. Viewing almost everyone as a potential friend, Rostov is quick to find the things he has in common with others, seeing their shared humanity rather than differences of class, age, nationality or political persuasion. Thus he bonds with Abram, the hotel handyman, over nostalgic memories of their place of birth and with Osip, a Communist Head of Security, over a love of lively debate and a mutual admiration of Humphrey Bogart. The Count's friendships cross class, political, national and generational divisions, allowing him to recognise kindred spirits in Nina, a nine-year-old girl, as well as Richard

Vanderwhile, an American aide-de-camp. Meanwhile, his ability to reconsider first impressions leads to a 'friends with benefits' relationship with movie star Anna Urbanova.

Much more than passing acquaintanceships, the Count's friendships endure over the years. While his bond with long-time friend Mishka remains as strong as ever, despite lengthy periods apart, Count Rostov also forges new ones. The way his relationship with Andrey and Emile is shown to slowly grow from a civil one between hotel guest and staff to unshakeable Triumvirate conveys the way the bonds of friendship strengthen over time through mutual respect and trust.

Coming second only to parental love in the novel, friendship is shown to be the source of breath-taking acts of generosity on a number of occasions. While taken aback at Nina's sudden arrival with Sofia, the Count never considers refusing his friend's request to look after her daughter. Similarly, Viktor risks his own life (as well as the wrath of his wife) to help the Count escape Moscow. Meanwhile Osip risks professional ruin when he makes arrangements for Sofia's medical care and helps to cover up the Count's temporary absence from the Metropol. The nurturing of international friendship also proves to be vitally useful for the Count when Richard Vanderwhile ensures the smooth-running of Sofia's defection from the American Embassy in exchange for a 'favour' from his Russian friend.

IMAGERY

A charming characteristic of *A Gentleman in Moscow* is the way seemingly incidental objects appear and then reappear in a different context. *The Essays of Montaigne* are adapted from tedious reading matter to handy desk leveller to secret repository of gold coins. The 'Fountain of Youth' is an intriguing elixir in the hotel barber's cabinet, later revealing itself to be hair dye when Sofia uses it to cover the distinctive white steak in her hair. The egret-shaped scissors are a decorative reminder of the Count's beloved sister, later used for the practical purpose of cutting Sofia's hair short enough to disguise her as a boy. A hand bell in the shape of a lady (the silver summoner) is a novelty discovered by Nina and the Count on one of their first adventures which makes a reappearance during the Count's last dinner with Sofia. In this way, ordinary objects prove as adaptable as the Count himself, constantly transforming themselves to meet the needs of new situations.

The Antique Dueling Pistols

The existence of the antique dueling pistols is first mentioned when the Count tells Nina about a duel his godfather took part in while staying at the hotel. A legendary part of the Metropol's history, the guns were kept behind a secret panel by the manager in the days when arguments between aristocratic guests would be settled by a duel. When Manager Halecki informs the Count that his staff can no longer address him by his title, Rostov makes the best of the situation, checking that the pistols still lie behind the secret panel in his office. This knowledge comes in very useful later when the Count prevents the Bishop from reporting him to the authorities at gunpoint.

More than just a handy plot device, the dueling pistols symbolise the Count's aristocratic background and a way of life that has become obsolete. When the Bishop at first dismisses the pistols as harmless antiques, the Count proves he is mistaken by firing a shot into Stalin's portrait. Perfectly at ease with how to handle these reminders of his aristocratic past, the Count proves that, like the pistols themselves, he is far from powerless and should not be underestimated.

The Grand Duke's Desk

When the Count is forced to choose which of his possessions to cram into his attic room, one of his first selections is his Louis XVI desk. Inherited from his godfather, the desk has come to represent those qualities which the Count most admired in the Grand Duke, who became a mentor to him after his parents died. A military hero, the Grand Duke "prized industry over nonsense" and gave the Count the valuable advice that "if a man does not master his circumstances then he is bound to be mastered by them." The marks etched into the desk's surface reflect the previous owner's industrious nature and sense of purpose while the hollow legs conveniently conceal gold coins.

The Twice-tolling Clock

The twice-tolling clock is another prized possession salvaged by the Count for his attic room. Unique in only chiming twice a day (at noon and midnight) the clock was designed to support his father's theories about how a day should be valuably spent. While the Count adheres less and less to his father's maxim of working only until noon and ensuring that he is asleep before midnight, the clock is a reminder of the passage of time and a prompt to spend it purposefully.

Opera Glasses

The Count keeps a pair of mother-of-pearl opera glasses to remind him of their former owner, his grandmother. Like the antique dueling pistols and "all manner of carefully crafted things that have outlived their usefulness", the glasses are also a reminder of a way of life which has become extinct. As with many objects in the novel, however, the glasses prove to have a new use when the Count presents them to Nina as a Christmas gift. Perfect for Nina's inquisitive nature, the thoughtful gift proves how well Count Rostov knows his young friend.

Hotel Passkey

The hotel passkey Nina wears around her neck is a symbol of her adventurous and enquiring nature. It is this key that opens up many of the secret wonders of the Metropol to the Count, making his house arrest far more bearable. When Nina gives the key to the Count as a Christmas gift it allows him to continue roaming the hotel freely in her absence. Possession of it becomes crucial later in the novel when the Count accumulates the items Sofia needs to defect.

Casablanca

When the Count and Osip watch 'Casablanca' together, as with many of the scenes in the novel, the episode has more significance than is at first apparent. First there are the similarities between the setting of the classic movie and the situation the Count finds himself in. In the film, the French Moroccan city is a popular destination for Europeans seeking to escape the Second World War. Here, travellers wait to obtain visas to the New World in a strange kind of limbo. Within this setting, Rick's Café is a pleasant oasis, sharply contrasting with its surroundings. Like the Hotel Metropol, the American-style café attracts customers who wish to experience a little comfort and luxury while forgetting about the turbulent events taking place outside its walls. Osip suggests that the Count likes the movie so much because both he and Humphrey Bogart wear a white dinner jacket to serve their customers. Count Rostov also shares something in common with the café customers however, as his house arrest places him in a similar state of limbo.

One of the famous scenes of the movie generates a great deal of discussion between Osip and the Count. This is the moment when a petty criminal, Ugarte, is seized by guards in the café and implores Rick (played by Humphrey Bogart) to help him. Rick stands 'impassively' as Ugarte is taken away, urges his customers to continue enjoying themselves and tells the pianist, Sam, to continue playing. Osip, who is a great believer that progress can only be achieved by ruthlessness, particularly admires the 'indifference' Rick demonstrates when he carries on as normal as Ugarte is taken away. The Count, however, is troubled by this interpretation of the scene.

Later in the novel, when Viktor and the Count meet in a café, a pastiche of the famous scene in 'Casablanca' takes place before their eyes. After two fruit sellers are thrown off the premises for fighting, the resident accordion player strikes up a tune to restore harmony. Reminded of his favourite movie, the Count describes the relevant scene to Viktor and Osip's interpretation of it. When Viktor watches the film a year later, he remembers his conversation with the Count and notes that, in the scene in question, Rick sets right an upturned cocktail glass as he walks away from the fracas. Observing this detail, Viktor realises that Rick is not displaying indifference to his fellow man but a desire to put in order those small things that he has the power to change. This astute character analysis does, of course, equally apply to the Count.

Food & Drink

Count Rostov is a connoisseur of fine food and wine and his refined palate is reflected in the novel's sensuous descriptions of food and drink. For the Count, food is much more than a necessity as he savours each individual flavour of a simple breakfast, from the tartness of an apple to the contrasting sweetness of his biscuit. The ability of food and drink to evoke memories and places is also emphasised in the novel. When the Count first tastes the honey from Abram's bees he is transported to the Alexander Gardens where the bees have been feeding on the lilacs.

Eating is presented as one of life's great joys and the powerful impact food can have upon human emotions is demonstrated on a number of occasions. When the Triumvirate gather together in the early hours of the morning to eat their long-awaited bouillabaisse, they also open up their hearts to each other, revealing new and unexpected details about themselves. Meanwhile, on the brink of suicide, the Count realises that his life is worth living when he tastes the honey produced from the apple trees of Nizhny Novgorod.

The Count's appreciation of food and wine directly contrasts with that of the Bishop. The Bishop's joyless attitude towards life in general is reflected in his inability to grasp the importance of selecting wine that complements a meal. When he recommends a completely inappropriate wine to a young couple, the Count cannot help but intervene, recognising that the choice could prove disastrous for the couple's romantic future. In an act of spiteful retaliation, the Bishop then ensures that the hotel's extensive wine selection is banned, offering its customers only the sobering choice of red or white.

The Bishop's attitude towards food and drink reflects the ideology of a Soviet Communist Party that inflicted austerity and even famine on its people while enjoying luxuries unavailable to normal citizens. It is no accident that Mishka's falling out with the Party involves a literary reference to food. Already angry at being forced to delete Chekov's innocuous praise of German bread from one of his letters, it is the final straw for Mishka when he sees the man responsible for the censorship sharing a cheese platter with his colleagues. His rebellion is to produce a compilation of literary references to bread, concluding with the censored Chekov quote.

The instruction to remove the labels from the Metropol's bottles of wine is a similar act of pointless and petty censorship on the part of the Communist regime. By ensuring that the wines have no labels, the Bolsheviks deliberately remove their individual identities. This process has much in common with their attempt to erase the Count's identity by stripping him of his title and declaring him a 'former person'. Like Mishka, however, the Count offers up a small act of resistance by identifying a bottle of Châteauneuf-du-Pape from the thousands of blank bottles in the cellar. In doing so he demonstrates that, try as they might, the state cannot erase individualism altogether.

Matryoshka Dolls

When the Count lets himself into the suite of an Italian couple, searching for suitable clothes for Sofia's escape, he finds a set of matryoshka dolls in their closet. The Russian dolls are just one of a number of objects in the novel that are designed to conceal something else inside. When the Count opens his Christmas gift from Nina, he finds boxes within boxes until the final and smallest reveals the hotel passkey: an object specifically designed for revealing secret things. Other examples of objects hidden inside other objects include the gold coins hidden in the legs of the Grand Duke's desk and later inside *The Essays of Montaigne;* the room hidden in the back of a closet; the dueling pistols behind a secret panel and a top-secret document sewn into the lining of a knapsack. This array of objects with hidden purposes reflects the structure of Towles' novel in which a series of incidents only reveal their relationship to each other by the end.

CHARACTERS

A Gentleman in Moscow boasts a cast of colourful characters. While a handful of the minor characters are real historical figures, the central characters are fictional.

Count Alexander Ilyich Rostov

The gentleman of the novel's title is Count Rostov and, although the story is told through a third-person narrative, the Count's perspective is the main focus. How much a reader enjoys *A Gentleman in Moscow* will very much depend upon their reaction to the Count as a character. Those who find him charming (as the author clearly intends) will emotionally invest in the Count's experiences. Readers who are less appreciative of his character quirks will find the story less engaging.

At the beginning of the novel a transcript of the Count's appearance before a Bolshevik tribunal establishes Rostov as a nineteenth century Russian aristocrat who is out-of-tune with a hostile twentieth century world. He does himself no favours with the court by unapologetically declaring himself to be "recipient of the Order of Saint Andrew", "member of the Jockey Club" and "Master of the Hunt." While these attributes are anathema to his Bolshevik audience, for the Count they are as much a part of his identity as his name. Continuing to dig his own grave, the Count adds that, as a gentleman can't possibly work for a living, he spends his time, "Dining, discussing. Reading, reflecting." While these statements should be enough to seal his fate in Communist Russia, the Count is saved from execution by virtue of a poem he wrote before the Revolution entitled 'Where Is It Now?' Thanks to the apparently pro-revolutionary message of this poem, he is sentenced to house arrest in the Metropol Hotel instead.

When the Count is returned to the Metropol, however, it is as a different person to the one who left it. Now a 'former person' rather than an aristocrat, he is moved from his grand suite to an obscure attic room. His usual gentlemanly routines (mornings in his favourite bakery, lunch at the Jockey Club, afternoons sat in the Alexander Gardens and "chance encounters with young ladies of fashion") are completely curtailed as he is unable to step outside the doors of the hotel. It is at this point that Amor Towles' choice of title for his novel becomes truly meaningful. The Count is a gentleman not because of his aristocratic background but because of the way he conducts himself when faced with unwelcome change.

While it can't be denied that the Count possesses certain qualities that are the product of a privileged upbringing (e.g. his refined taste in food, wine and literature), it is his personality that defines him as a true gentleman. As well as wit and intelligence, he demonstrates impeccable manners, no matter what the circumstances. Shoe-horned into a cramped attic room, he nevertheless extends as warm a welcome to Andrey, Vasily and Marina as if he were hosting a dinner at Idlehour. The genuine courtesy he extends to everyone he meets, no matter what their social standing, leads him to forge lasting friendships across class, political and generational boundaries. The Count also continually displays grace under pressure, brilliantly illustrated in his unruffled response when an angry man snips off his moustache.

Most striking in the Count's reaction to his reduced circumstances is his surprising resilience and sense of optimism. While using his ingenuity to acquire little luxuries such as a mille-feuille from his favourite bakery, he makes the most of those things he cannot change, comparing his cramped new living quarters to the small berths on boats and trains that he longed to sleep in as a boy. Although deprived of the opportunity to meet young ladies and socialise with members of the Jockey Club, he still finds rewarding company in the form of hotel staff members and guests.

Count Rostov's determination to find new sources of pleasure and maintain his gentlemanly standards go a long way to make his house arrest more bearable. Nevertheless, as the years pass by, he begins to feel that the Bolsheviks have succeeded in erasing his identity. Unable to leave the four walls of the hotel, he remains in a state of limbo while witnessing change all around him. Familiar members of staff are replaced with strange faces; his young friend, Nina, grows up and moves out of the hotel; Mishka becomes increasingly absorbed in his busy work and love life, and even

Abram's bees leave the hotel roof for fresh pastures.

Added to Count Rostov's increasing sense of purposelessness is his guilt over the fate of his sister, Helena. Blaming himself for the chain of events that led to his sister's humiliation and his inability to be present when she died, he resolves to kill himself on the tenth anniversary of her death. His suicide attempt is interrupted, however, by the discovery that the bees have returned to the Metropol. The realisation that the bees have travelled hundreds of miles to return with nectar from the apple blossom of Nizhny Novgorod proves enough to give the Count a reason to live. It is at this point in the novel that the Count realises the importance of a sense of purpose.

Count Rostov's newly purposeful life begins when he is transformed from a regular diner in the Boyarsky restaurant to Head Waiter. In this role his refined palate allows him to make perfectly judged recommendations to the diners while his intuitive understanding of etiquette and social nuances makes him a "master of seating tables". Able to conjure up a wine suitable for every dish and budget, he also meticulously checks reservations to ensure that rival members of the Communist Party are not seated near one another. Having stated at the beginning of the novel that gentlemen do not work for a living, the Count discovers real satisfaction in using his talents to serve others. By bringing everything he has to the role, he experiences the satisfaction of true purposefulness.

Having thoroughly embraced the rewards of a working life, the Count discovers an even greater sense of purpose when he becomes a father. When Sofia is placed in his care, Count Rostov initially feels inconvenienced by the role as it hopelessly complicates both his working and social life. It does not take him long, however, to make the transition from bachelor to doting father. Coming to welcome the 'inconveniences' of parenthood, the Count's final challenge is to let Sofia go. Realising that he is in danger of limiting her horizons by keeping her at the hotel, he urges her to begin a new life without him, despite his pain at losing her. To do so, he also shows that he is willing to sacrifice his principles for his daughter, retracting his vow that he will never act as a spy for the Americans in order to arrange Sofia's defection.

Nina Kulikova

As a nine-year-old girl Nina bulldozes her way into Count Rostov's life when she approaches his table demanding to know where his moustaches have gone. The Count does not initially welcome the child's impertinent and interrogative conversational style (apparently inspired by conversations Amor Towles had with his own daughter). As it turns out, however, Nina provides a much-needed breath of fresh air in the Count's stale life. In their regular "excursions", she reignites Rostov's childlike sense of fun while also opening up a whole new aspect of the hotel to him. The passkey she wears around her neck (and eventually bestows upon the Count) gives them free rein to roam the Metropol and reveals unexpected delights.

The opera glasses the Count presents to Nina for Christmas are a symbol of her curious nature. Once a subject takes her fancy, she makes it her mission to investigate every aspect of it – from her determination to discover everything there is to know about the lives of princesses to the interest she takes in the proceedings of the Bolshevik Assemblies. An independent thinker, Nina never accepts something as the truth simply because it is presented to her as a fact. This is illustrated in her refusal to accept that she should say thank you when presented with something she hasn't asked for and in her insistence upon testing out the established theories of famous mathematicians.

Nina's fascination with the lives of royalty is shown to be ironic when she later transfers her allegiances to the Communist Party. When, after several years of absence, the Count spots her in the lobby of the Metropol, he realises she has joined the Komsomol (a youth organisation of the Communist Party). Explaining that she is about to leave for the countryside to aid in the collectivization of farming, Nina speaks of the "historical necessity" of Stalin's five-year-plan with the same intensity that she once applied to her scientific and mathematical studies. While the Count is pleased to see that Nina remains as confident and passionate as ever, he notes with some regret that her political convictions have made her "humourless" and are standing in the way of her indulging in youthful pleasures. Nina's transition from fun-loving adventurer to sober comrade is emphasised by the drab Bolshevik uniform she wears, which starkly contrasts with the cheerful yellow dresses she favoured as a child.

Nina's mission ends in political disillusionment and personal heartbreak. By witnessing first-hand the human suffering caused by Stalin's collectivization of agriculture (both to the resident farmers forced off their land and to the millions who die of starvation), Nina realises that her faith in the Communist Party has been misplaced. This is confirmed when her husband, Leo, is arrested and sentenced to five years of labour in Sevvostlag. Considering Count Rostov to be the one friend she can rely on, she leaves her young daughter, Sofia, with him, intending to return for her when she has found a job and somewhere to live close to where her husband has been sent. Her failure to ever return suggests that she too becomes a victim of the Communist Party's harsh justice system.

Sofia

Nina's daughter, Sofia, is between five and six years old when she comes to live at the Metropol. At first, Count Rostov is intimidated by her quiet, serious manner. At a loss as how to entertain her, he suggests a game of find the thimble. When she repeatedly outwits him at this game, the Count realises he has underestimated the little girl's keen intelligence.

Less intense than her mother, Sofia combines Nina's love of knowledge with a "playful streak", illustrated by the incident when she releases geese into the hotel corridors and by her love of surprising the Count by anticipating his whereabouts and lying in wait for him. Her ability to disappear and then reappear in a different part of the hotel shows that she is just as familiar with the Metropol's hidden corridors and connecting doors as her mother once was.

Sofia pays the Count the ultimate compliment when she addresses him as "my guardian angel, my father, and my friend". As she grows older, however, her devotion to Count Rostov makes her determined to remain in the hotel with him, potentially restricting her life's prospects. Only on the Count's insistence does she finally agree to leave for Paris and a new life. The moment when she stops to admire the illuminated Arc de Triomphe and the Louvre on her hurried way to the American Embassy symbolises the many new wonders she is to discover.

Anna Urbanova

Anna Urbanova is in her mid-twenties when the Count first sees her in the lobby of the Metropol. "Willowy" and strikingly attractive, the movie star's appearance is enhanced by the two sleek borzois she has on a leash – until they cause chaos by chasing the one-eyed cat through the lobby. The Count restores order with a whistle but is unimpressed by the woman's haughty manner. He is forced to reassess his first impression of Anna, however, when she invites him up to her room for dinner and demonstrates impressive skills when deboning a fish.

Accustomed to getting her own way, Anna takes the Count to bed and then rudely dismisses him in the early hours of the morning. When he stops to hang up her blouse before departing, however, she feels it to be a silent reproach of her carelessness. The incident bothers her for weeks and, as an act of rebellion against Count Rostov, throws her clothes on the floor at her home in St. Petersburg until her dresser threatens to spank her. Her pride once again piqued, Anna throws the clothes out into the street, only to realise the foolishness of her actions and creep outside to retrieve them. This scene was inspired by a real-life incident between Amor Towles' parents in the early days of their marriage, when his mother refused to pick up her clothes and his father responded by throwing them out the window.

Anna's career is subject to the political changes taking place in the Soviet Union. As a young actress, she appears in the films of a director whose work emphasised the virtues of the working classes and the corruption of the aristocracy. As these movies initially received the seal of approval from the Communist Party, Anna became a star and was given a luxuriously furnished mansion. As the ideology of the party changed, however, the films fell out of favour and were judged to be too nostalgic and individualistic. The development of the talking picture also proved disastrous for the unfashionably husky-voiced actress. A 'has-been' at twenty-nine, her mansion is confiscated and she is reduced to attempting to seduce directors into giving her minor roles. Her career is revived, however, when a devoted admirer of hers becomes Minister of Culture.

Anna's chequered career history, from star to has-been and back again, demonstrates her tenacity and also her ability to adapt to and make the best of changing circumstances. By her fifties she has made a successful transition to the stage. Realising that the theatre is more flattering for an ageing beauty than movie close-ups, she draws upon her life experience to play great roles such as Lady Macbeth and Medea. The changes in her circumstances also lead to a change in her character as she casts off her pride and egotism to join "the Confederacy of the Humbled." Like the Count, she realises that good fortune and privilege can be fleeting and it is the way that one responds to bad times that truly demonstrates character. No longer interested in playing power games with the Count, she settles into a more honest relationship with him – symbolised by her admission that she lied about her father being a fisherman.

Anna's intelligence and wit make her a perfect companion for the Count. His intellectual equal, she keeps him on his toes with good-humoured teasing and isn't afraid to point out when he is being old-fashioned or ridiculous.

Panteleimon Nachevko (The Round-faced Commissar)

Generally referred to in the novel as the "round-faced Commissar" Panteleimon Nachevko is the Director of Cinematographic Arts in Moscow when he first meets Anna Urbanova. His infatuation with her proves very useful over the years as he becomes increasingly influential within the Communist government. Finally promoted to the powerful position of Minister of Culture, he holds significant power over the careers of all Russian artists. As well as reviving Anna's flagging acting career, he is responsible, at Anna's request, for securing Sofia a position in the Moscow Conservatory, saving her from being forced to join an orchestra in Stalingrad 600 miles away. Rumours that Anna is Nachevko's long-standing mistress also prevent difficult questions being asked about Sofia's presence at the Metropol, as Communist Party members assume that she is the minister's illegitimate daughter. While it is clear that Anna encourages the attentions of this influential man, the novel's narrator is too gentlemanly to ever spell out the true nature of their relationship.

Mikhail Fyodorovich Mindich (Mishka)

Count Rostov and his lifelong friend, Mishka, are as different as chalk and cheese. While the Count grew up in a twenty-room mansion with fourteen staff, Mishka was raised by his mother in a small apartment. While the Count is known for his easy charm, wit and impeccable grooming, Mishka is distinguished by his habit of restlessly pacing, his seriousness and his ragged beard. Most crucially, while Rostov, as an aristocrat, is a casualty of the Russian Revolution, Mishka is a supporter of it. Nevertheless, the two men are like brothers, demonstrating the many boundaries that friendship is capable of crossing.

Mishka's appearances in the novel emphasise how the Count's house arrest places him in limbo. When they were at university together, Count Rostov was the one with the colourful social life while Mishka preferred to stay in and study, happy to experience life vicariously through his friend's anecdotes. These roles are reversed, however, when the Count is stuck in the Metropol and can only wait for his friend to visit with tales of the outside world. Although Mishka remains a devoted friend, his visits become less frequent as his life is overtaken by work and romance. The Count increasingly finds himself dining alone as Mishka is called to literary meetings or rushes off to pursue Katerina, the woman he has fallen in love with.

Mishka's intermittent appearances also provide a telling portrait of post-revolutionary Russia. When we first meet him, Mishka is in Moscow to attend the Russian Association of Proletarian Writers and expresses great excitement at the changes he believes the Communist Party will usher in. These include an end to the oppression of the working classes, technological advances and freedom of artistic expression. At first, things appear to be going well for Mishka as his romance with Katerina blossoms and he embarks on exciting literary projects. Gradually, however, he undergoes a process of disillusionment as he is cast aside by Katerina and the Communist government proves to be far more oppressive than he anticipated. Matters come to a head when, after working on a volume of Anton Chekhov's letters for years, he is instructed to delete a passage in which the Russian playwright enthusiastically praises the bread in Berlin. After he makes a scene in public, Mishka's actions are brought to the attention of the authorities and he is sent to Siberia to complete eight years of hard labour. Mishka's ravaged appearance when he illegally reappears in Moscow is a testament to the severity of his punishment. The Count also notices that his friend refers to himself as 'we' – a consequence of being herded along like livestock with many others in the Gulag.

Shortly after Mishka dies, Katerina arrives at the Metropol to break the news to the Count and present him with his friend's most recent literary project. Entitled *Bread and Salt* the book is a compendium of quotations about bread taken from famous literary works, ending with the sentence that Mishka was instructed to cut from Chekov's letter. This work of literary rebellion proves that, despite his experiences, Mishka's spirit was never entirely broken. It is at this point that the Count reveals to Katerina that Mishka was the true author of the revolutionary poem, 'Where Is It Now?'

Osip Ivanovich Glebnikov

The Count first meets Osip when he is summoned to a private function at the hotel to find a single diner waiting for him. A brutal scar above the man's left ear suggests that he has been the subject of at least one assassination attempt, and he introduces himself as Osip Ivanovich Glebnikov, former colonel of the Red Army. Osip explains that, as Russia is at a crucial point in its relations with other countries, it is important that he understands the society, culture and languages of these nations. He asks the Count to dine with him once a month to educate him on these matters.

While the Count has little choice but to accept the former colonel's request, their meetings prove surprisingly agreeable for both parties. Although holding completely different views, the two men enjoy the cut and thrust of their debates and develop a mutual respect for each other. When their syllabus turns to American film, Osip is shown to be completely immersed in the spectacle of Hollywood glitz, acting out fight scenes and dances as he watches them, before declaring them "shameful" pieces of propaganda. Of all their discussions, however, the Count is troubled by one in particular - Osip's interpretation of 'Casablanca'. In the famous scene when Humphrey Bogart instructs the pianist to keep playing after a man is dragged from the café by police, Osip sees ruthless indifference in Bogart's behaviour. His admiration of the character's apparent lack of sentiment reflects his belief that the Soviet Union will only become a world power by ruthlessly casting aside the old in favour of the new.

Osip's promotion to Chief Administrator of Security in the Kremlin proves that his lessons with the Count, combined with his ruthlessly ambitious drive, have paid off. Some of his actions, however, prove that he is not as indifferent to the fates of others as he likes to think. When Sofia has her accident he proves to be a true friend to the Count when he uses his influence to make sure that the best surgeon in Moscow operates on her. He also compromises his professional integrity when he ensures that the Count returns to the hotel before anyone realises he has broken the terms of his house arrest. Later, when he receives news of the Count's escape and Sofia's defection, the smile he suppresses indicates that, within his steely exterior lies a sentimental heart. He also demonstrates that he has come to appreciate some of the Count's values when he observes that the Count didn't shoot the hotel manager when he had the chance, "because Leplevsky isn't an aristocrat."

Richard Vanderwhile

The Count first makes the acquaintance of Richard Vanderwhile when he stays in the Metropol as aide-de-camp to an American general. Despite the suspicion with which their nations view each other, the Russian Count quickly identifies the American as a kindred spirit with similar tastes and beliefs.

After a conversation with the Count about Russia's ruthless attitude to its heritage in the pursuit of progress, Richard offers the comforting theory that "grand things persist" even in the face of great change. He backs up this argument by giving the Count a phonograph along with a recording of the Russian pianist, Vladimir Horowitz, playing Tchaikovsky's First Piano Concerto at Carnegie Hall to rapturous applause. This unexpected gift seems to have a twofold message. The Tchaikovsky recording proves that great Russian heritage not only persists but is appreciated across the world. As Vladimir Horowitz defected during a tour of Berlin, the gift is also a reminder that Russian citizenship is something that can be cast aside if necessary.

While Richard's promotion to the State Department means that he stays at the Embassy rather than the Metropol when in Moscow, he still drops into the hotel to indulge in a brightly-coloured cocktail with the Count and their friendship endures over the years. In 1952, after being promoted to a role in the American Embassy in Paris, Richard tells the Count that the American government are eager to glean information on who is likely to become the next Soviet leader when Stalin dies. Count Rostov is adamant that he is not prepared to become a spy and the matter appears to be closed. When Sofia defects from her Paris tour and takes sanctuary with Richard at the American Embassy it becomes clear that the Count changed his mind.

Jozef Halecki

The hotel manager at the beginning of the novel, Mr. Halecki has "mastered the secret of delegation". While projecting a harried manner in public, the well-worn chaise longue is testament to his predilection for afternoon naps. Although Halecki has to inform Count Rostov that members of his staff are no longer permitted to call him 'Your Excellency', he takes no pleasure in the task.

Comrade Leplevsky (The Bishop)

Although his real name is finally revealed to be Leplevsky, this character is better known as 'the Bishop'. Count Rostov privately gives him this name when he reflects that the man's tall and thin frame, "narrow head and superior demeanor" make him look like this particular chess piece. During the Count's house arrest at the Metropol, the Bishop experiences a meteoric rise from incompetent waiter to hotel manager.

When the Bishop first waits on the Count's table in the Piazza, Count Rostov notes that the Bishop's entire manner is at odds with the ethos of the Metropol's staff. Incompetent and unhelpful, he gives the impression that serving others is beneath him. The Count's conviction that the Bishop does not understand the higher purpose of being a waiter is confirmed when he observes him recommend an expensive and inappropriate wine for a young couple's meal. Unable to watch the young couple's date descend into disaster, the Count cannot help but intervene, recommending a wine more sympathetic to their meal and the young man's budget. This intervention is to prove costly, however, for by undermining the Bishop's professional integrity, the Count makes himself a dangerous enemy. From this point, the Bishop makes it his mission to disrupt the Count's pleasures at every opportunity. This begins with his recommendation that diners should only be offered red or white wine, leading to the removal of all labels on the wine bottles in the cellar.

Unfortunately for Count Rostov, the Bishop clearly has friends (or relatives) in high places within the Communist Party - the only possible explanation for his promotion from Piazza waiter to hotel manager. His close connections with the Party are reflected in the changes he makes to the manager's office, where Halecki's chaise longue is replaced by locked filing cabinets and the traditional hunting scenes on the walls are superseded by portraits of Stalin, Lenin and Marx. Unsurprisingly, the Bishop's management style exemplifies all the most unpleasant characteristics of the Russian Communist government. Oppressive and watchful, he keeps secret files on the character flaws of his guests and staff while unnecessarily interfering with every aspect of hotel life. By introducing interminable paperwork in the restaurant to eliminate "discrepancies", he ensures that meals arrive cold at the tables, while his penny-pinching changes to the menu cramp Emile's culinary talents. Humourless and officious, he erodes the morale of his staff and makes the Metropol a less pleasant place to stay for its guests.

Like many warring heroes and arch-villains, the Count and the Bishop are represented as polar opposites. Although both are men of purpose, Count Rostov finds fulfilment in serving others, while the Bishop dedicates himself to eliminating joy from the lives of those around him. Count Rostov's natural charm and wit contrast sharply with the Bishop's misanthropic attitude and lack of humour. The ongoing battle of wits between these two opposites has obvious parallels with a protracted game of chess. The game finally ends in checkmate when Count Rostov arms himself with the antique duelling pistols, regaining the upper-hand. When the Bishop is forced to hand over the keys to his filing cabinets at gunpoint, he relinquishes all appearance of authority and his self-important manner dissolves. He suffers the final indignity when the Count locks him in a store cupboard.

Emile Zhukovsky

The head chef of the hotel's Boyarsky restaurant, Emile is both admired and feared. While many people find him abrupt and the kitchen staff lives in fear of his fiery temper, he is also an undisputed culinary genius, able to turn the most meagre ingredients into a dish fit for royalty. A depressive in most other aspects of his life, Emile comes alive in his kitchen, finding both meaning and purpose in his work. His softer side is gradually revealed as the Count's professional relationship with him becomes a friendship over the years.

Andrey Duras

The maître d' of the Boyarsky restaurant, Andrey is a consummate professional, intuiting the every need of his diners. Andrey's physical poise is humorously emphasised in a comparison between the elegant way in which he points to menu recommendations and the hand of God depicted by Michelangelo on the Sistine Chapel. Like Count Rostov, he always displays grace under pressure and believes that even the smallest tasks should be performed with care and pride.

Andrey demonstrates that we should never underestimate those we think we know when, after many years of working with Count Rostov and Emile, he reveals that he joined a travelling circus at the age of sixteen. He then demonstrates his superb juggling skills with oranges and knives. Later, Andrey's reputation as a safe pair of hands seems in jeopardy when he announces that he is suffering from palsy. Only when the Count escapes from the Metropol does the maître d' reveal to Emile that he faked a tremor to ensure that Rostov oversaw the all-important state dinner.

While Andrey is a minor character for much of the novel, Towles chooses to present a small section of the narrative from his point-of-view. After visiting Sofia in hospital on behalf of the Count, he returns to the apartment he shares with his wife. Although the apartment is small, the former bedroom of Ilya, their only child who was killed in the Battle of Berlin, is kept like a shrine. This poignant insight into Andrey's life outside the hotel demonstrates the private tragedies that many ordinary people stoically carry around.

Marina Samarova

The Count's initial assessment of the Metropol's seamstress as a "shy delight" is shown to be humorously misguided as he gets to know her better. Their acquaintance begins as the Count is called to use her services after splitting his trousers during his escapades with Nina. As time goes on, however, and the Count becomes more self-sufficient, she teaches him to sew and they often sit stitching together companionably. Never afraid to speak her mind, Marina tells the Count off for his trouser malfunctions and accuses him of being old-fashioned when he criticises the "dressless dress" she designs for Sofia. She also makes it very clear that the Count cannot cast her in the role as a permanent babysitter for young Sofia, emphasising that it is he who is responsible for mothering her. Marina's personality is reflected in her good and her wandering eye, one of which bears a grave expression while the other sparkles with humour.

Abram

The Count strikes up a friendship with Abram, the hotel handyman, when he first explores the roof of the Metropol. Abram reveals an unexpected wonder to the Count in the form of his bees. After this, the two men meet on the roof regularly to drink coffee, nostalgically discuss Nizhny Novgorod (where they were both born) and identify the bees' travels from the taste of their honey. Abram plays a crucial part in the story when he interrupts the Count's suicide attempt to share the good news that the bees have returned to the roof after a lengthy absence. When the Count discovers that their honey bears the unmistakable taste of Nizhny Novgorod's apple blossoms, his appetite for life is reawakened.

Arkady

Arkady is the hotel's "unflappable" desk manager.

Audrius

The Lithuanian bartender of the Shalyapin, Audrius is attentive and efficient.

Vasily

The hotel's concierge, Vasily, has the magical power to conjure up theatre tickets for sold-out performances if guests require them.

Yaroslav Yaroslavl

Another talented member of the Metropol's team, Yaroslav Yaroslavl is the maestro of all barbers. Working with two sets of scissors at once, he cuts hair with unparalleled elegance and speed. He is also the original curator of the cabinet admired by the Count, displaying tonics, soaps and 'the Fountain of Youth'.

Viktor Stepanovich Skadovsky

When Sofia is seventeen, Count Rostov is horrified to find her apparently canoodling with the conductor of the Piazza's orchestra, Viktor Stepanovich Skadovsky. The Count's instinctive paternal response is to grab Viktor by the lapels before Sofia can explain that he is teaching her to play the piano. A talented musician trained at the Moscow Conservatory, Viktor has taken the conducting job in the restaurant to support his wife and two children.

As it turns out, Viktor proves to be an extremely positive presence in the lives of Sofia and the Count. Selflessly nurturing Sofia's talent, it is he who gives her the opportunity to join the Moscow Conservatory. He also risks his life by acting as a decoy, giving the Count the chance to escape Moscow. Viktor's courageous actions are motivated by his moral conviction that it is the right thing to do and also the great respect he feels for Count Rostov. This respect is reflected in the fact that Viktor continues to call the Count "Your Excellency" long after others have abandoned this nicety. Viktor uses this title not because he is in awe of the Count's aristocratic background, but because he feels it reflects Rostov's essential nobility of character. This admiration for the Count's gentlemanly conduct is demonstrated in Viktor's response to the controversial scene in 'Casablanca'. Noting that Humphrey Bogart sets right an upturned cocktail glass as he walks away from a fracas, Viktor is reminded of the Count's belief that small actions can make a difference in a sometimes unpleasant world.

Lieutenant Pulonov

Count Rostov first encounters Lieutenant Pulonov on the way to the 21st birthday party of a princess. The young Hussar demonstrates he is far from a gentleman when he runs the Count's carriage off the road in his troika. Later, when they turn up at the same party, the Count settles the score by beating Pulonov at cards and romancing the princess under his nose.

Pulonov takes his revenge on Count Rostov by courting his sister, Helena, and then breaking her heart in a deliberately humiliating manner. In response, the Count shoots Pulonov in the shoulder – a wound which doesn't immediately kill him but later proves fatal when he is unable to defend himself with the lame arm in battle. Count Rostov bitterly regrets his behaviour towards Pulonov because of the events it sets in motion. Forced to lie low in Paris when Pulonov's father files a complaint against him, the Count is out of the country when his sister dies of scarlet fever. The incident causes the Count to vow that he will never kill a fellow countryman again.

Helena

The Count's sister, Helena, is the source of many bitter-sweet memories for him. While he fondly remembers the companionable hours they spent together at Idlehour, he feels responsible for her heartbreak and mourns the fact that he wasn't with her when she died. By keeping Helena's portrait in his room, the Count ensures that he is constantly reminded of her. His decision to end his life on the tenth anniversary of Helena's death expresses the depth of his guilt and grief.

The Countess

From his memories we learn that the Count shared a close bond with his grandmother, the Countess. While other members of the Rostov family despaired of the Count's youthful rebellious behaviour, his grandmother took pleasure in hearing of his antics. Concern for his grandmother's welfare is the reason for the

Count's return to Russia from Paris. The Countess becomes one of the many Russian aristocrats to flee the country to start a new life.

Grand Duke Demidov

Count Rostov's godfather, the Grand Duke, was a military hero and represented the Tsar at the signing of the Treaty of Portsmouth which ended the Russo-Japanese War. When the Count loses his parents at the age of ten the Grand Duke becomes a mentor to him, offering the valuable advice that "if a man does not master his circumstances then he is bound to be mastered by them." This is a maxim the Count later comes to live by. When the Grand Duke dies he leaves his godson a Louis XVI desk. The scarred desktop acts as a reminder to the Count of the importance of industry and purpose while the hollow legs double as a secret safe.

Katerina Litvinova

Mishka falls hopelessly in love with Katerina when they both serve on the committee of the Congress of the Russian Association of Proletarian Writers. Despite Mishka's devotion, she eventually leaves him to marry another man. After her husband's death, however, she is briefly reunited with Mishka before he dies. She then travels to Moscow to inform the Count of his friend's death and give him the manuscript of *Bread and Salt*.

The One-eyed Cat

The corridors of the Hotel Metropol are stalked by a "one-eyed Russian blue". After he is sentenced to house arrest, the Count begins to court the company of the cat with saucers of cream and dishes of ice cream. Although the cat doesn't have a name, the Count refers to the feline by various different titles according to the situation. As he watches the Count open his Christmas gift from Nina, the cat becomes 'Herr Drosselmeyer' (the magical inventor from *The Nutcracker* who sits on top of the grandfather clock. He then becomes 'Field Marshal Kutuzov' (the Russian officer whose troops forced Napoleon to retreat from Russia) when he fearlessly agitates Anna's dogs in the lobby.

Throughout the novel the cat acts as a silent yet judgemental witness of events. After being dismissed from Anna's bedroom in the early hours of the morning, the Count encounters the cat in the elevator and feels he views his humiliation with a stern expression. Years later, however, he encounters the cat's ghost immediately after locking the Bishop in a storeroom at gunpoint. To the Count's surprise, the cat shows no disappointment at his actions, thus giving his silent approval to the Count's escape.

Prince Nikolai Petrov

When Count Rostov recognises Prince Nikolai Petrov in the lobby of the Metropol, he arranges to meet him again for a drink the following Saturday. In a typically playful manner, however, the narrator advises the reader not to bother remembering the Prince's name, as he will not be keeping the appointment. Nevertheless, in a lengthy footnote the narrator invites the reader to emotionally invest in Prince Nikolai's life by describing precisely why he didn't meet Count Rostov as he had agreed. In this way, the narrator craftily ensures that readers remember the Prince, while urging them to forget him.

Prince Nikolai's fate provides a vivid illustration of the lives of ex-royalty and aristocracy in post-revolutionary Russia. Stripped of his royal privileges, he attempts to support himself as a jobbing musician. Work is almost impossible to come by, however, due to Communist restrictions upon hiring former royalty and Nikolai relies upon the kindness of his old music instructor, Sergei Eisenov, to secure him the occasional gig. After chancing upon the Count in the Metropol, however, the Prince returns home to find the secret police waiting for him. Arrested and sentenced for the possession of an old Latin grammar book containing a picture of Tsar Nicholas II, Prince Nikolai is presented with a 'Minus Six' permitting him to remain in Russia provided he never enters any of its six largest cities. His unfortunate music instructor, Sergei Eisenov, fares worse, being sent to a labour camp for hiring a 'former person' to play in his quartet.

Harrison Salisbury

When Amor Towles was ten years old, he threw a bottle containing a short note he had written into the Atlantic Ocean. A few weeks later he received a letter from the man who found it: Harrison Salisbury, the managing editor of *The New York Times*. From this childhood incident, a correspondence developed between Salisbury and Towles and they eventually met.

In his earlier career, Harrison Salisbury was the real-life chief correspondent for *The New York Times* in Moscow. The author of an important history of the Russian Revolution, *Black Nights, White Snow,* his memoirs were the source of some of the detail Towles uses in *A Gentleman in Moscow*. Salisbury's cameo appearance in the novel, along with the mention of his fedora and trench coat (stolen by the Count as a disguise) pay tribute to Salisbury's literary legacy on early twentieth century Russia as well as the author's serendipitous connection with him.

Stalin

In *A Gentleman in Moscow* Stalin only appears as Harrison Salisbury watches his coffin pass by the windows of Suite 317. His tyrannical presence is felt in the novel, however, by the references to 'Soso' (Stalin's nickname) and the descriptions of how his five-year-plan affected the Russian people. The five-mile queue of Russians observed by Harrison Salisbury paying their respects to the dead dictator demonstrates, however, that not all Russians considered him a tyrant. Some remembered him for leading the country's victory against Germany in World War II, while others respected him for his role in making the Soviet Union a world power.

Nikita Khrushchev

When Stalin died in 1953 a struggle for power began between several prominent members of the Communist Party, one of whom was Nikita Khrushchev. In *A Gentleman in Moscow*, Towles portrays a combined dinner of the Presidium and the Council of Ministers on 11 June 1954 as the crucial moment when Khrushchev emerged as the favourite for Soviet leader. When he dramatically reveals the capabilities of the new nuclear power plant in a piece of nicely judged theatrics, Khrushchev demonstrates that he is pulling the strings behind the entire occasion. In reality, Khrushchev emerged as the new leader in 1958 after several years of in-house wrangling within a collective leadership.

DISCUSSION QUESTIONS

1/ Discuss the style and tone of the novel's narrative voice. Why do you think the author chose to use an omniscient third-person narrator over the more obvious first-person narration of Count Rostov? Did you find the narrative voice effective?

2/ Spanning thirty-two years, the action of *A Gentleman in Moscow* takes place almost entirely within the Metropol Hotel. How does the author ensure that this single setting does not become tedious?

3/ In a review of *A Gentleman in Moscow* Ron Charles points out that "the whole enterprise depends on how deeply you fall in love with the Count." Did you fall in love with Count Rostov as a character? Why, or why not?

4/ Discuss the changes that occur in the Count's life when he becomes a 'Former Person'. How does he deal with these changes and what does this say about his character?

5/ Why did Amor Towles choose to call his novel *A Gentleman in Moscow* rather than 'A Count in Moscow'? What is it that makes Count Rostov a 'gentleman'? Do you think that many of the characteristics he displays have become obsolete in our modern world?

6/ Discuss the incident where Abram's bees return from their long journey to Nizhny Novgorod. Why does this moment prove to be a crucial turning point for the Count?

7/ The Count is known for his refined palate and food and drink play an important role in his life. How is this reflected in the descriptions of food in the novel? What associations are various foods shown to have? Why can't Count Rostov stop himself from interfering when he hears the Bishop recommend an entirely inappropriate wine to accompany a young couple's meal?

8/ Like many warring heroes and villains, Count Rostov and the Bishop are represented as complete opposites. Discuss their opposing character traits. In what respect does the Bishop's personality and behaviour mirror the ideology of the Soviet Communist government?

9/ Discuss the way work and purpose are portrayed in the novel. Do you agree with the implication that a sense of purpose is an essential ingredient for a fulfilling life?

10/ During his time at the Metropol the Count forges friendships which cross class, age and political boundaries. Discuss the friendships he makes and the things he finds in common with others. What is the novel's overall message about friendship?

11/ The classic movie 'Casablanca' is referred to on a number of occasions in *A Gentleman in Moscow*. What are the similarities between 'Casablanca' and Towles' novel? How does Osip interpret the famously misquoted 'play it again Sam' scene and in what way does Viktor's understanding of this scene differ? What does this tell us about their view of the world?

12/ Discuss how Sofia's arrival at the Metropol changes the life of the Count. How does he feel about these changes? Do you feel the novel offers an accurate insight into the experience of parenthood?

13/ Discuss the different ways in which the historical events taking place outside the Metropol are conveyed to the reader. Do these snippets of information tell us enough about the state of the Soviet Union during this period? Is the light tone of the novel at odds with the horrors of Stalinist Russia?

14/ Both Nina and Mishka have faith in the progress promised by the new Communist government but are eventually bitterly disillusioned. How do their experiences relate to the Count's fears about the relationship between progress and destruction?

15/ Discuss the way that time is represented in the novel – with particular reference to the novel's structure, and the symbolism of the twice-tolling clock. Do you agree with the Count's conclusion that we experience time differently as we grow older?

16/ On a first reading, the first half of the novel appears to describe a series of quirky but random encounters and objects. Only in the second half of the book does the significance of these encounters and objects become evident. Discuss some of the incidents or objects which seem to be incidental but prove highly significant to the story by the end of the novel. Did the apparent lack of narrative drive in the first half of the novel bother you, or were you happy to go with the flow? Was the narrative pay-off worth the wait?

17/ In her review of *A Gentleman in Moscow*, Annalisa Quinn comments that "Towles never lets anyone merely say goodbye when they could *bid adieu*, never puts a period where an exclamation point or dramatic ellipsis could stand." How did you feel about the author's delight in extravagant language?

18/ How did you interpret the ending of the novel? Did you find it a satisfactory conclusion to the story?

19/ Is there a danger that Towles' sympathetic portrayal of the Count glosses over the part many Russian aristocrats played in the oppression of the working classes?

20/ Given the choice, would you be happy to serve a lifetime sentence in the Metropol Hotel, or would you rather brave the outside world?

QUIZ QUESTIONS

1/ What is the Count's favourite novel?

2/ What is the name of the Rostov family estate?

3/ When the Count attempts to teach Nina the importance of good manners, what does she swear she will never do?

4/ The Count gives Nina his grandmother's opera glasses as a Christmas present. What does she give him in return?

5/ What is unique about the clock that the Count inherits from his father?

6/ After Anna dismisses the Count from her bed in the early hours of the morning, what does he do to particularly annoy her?

7/ What type of fruit grows abundantly in Nizhny Novgorod?

8/ How does Sofia transport three geese from the kitchen pantry to the fourth floor corridor of the hotel?

9/ When Sofia injures herself on the stairs, which character intervenes to ensure she receives the best medical attention?

10/ For which recipe do the Count, Andrey and Emile secretly collect 15 different ingredients?

11/ Who is Osip's favourite American actor?

12/ What does the Count dislike about the dress Marina makes for Sofia?

13/ Who is the author of the poem 'Where Is It Now?'

14/ What is 'the Fountain of Youth'?

15/ During the novel the Count hides gold coins in two different places. Name them.

QUIZ ANSWERS

1/ Anna Karenina

2/ Idlehour

3/ Say thank you for something she hasn't asked for

4/ The hotel passkey

5/ It only tolls twice a day: once at noon, once at midnight

6/ Hangs up her blouse before leaving

7/ Apples

8/ In the dumbwaiter

9/ Osip

10/ Bouillabaisse

11/ Humphrey Bogart

12/ It is backless

13/ Mishka

14/ Hair dye

15/ Within the legs of the Grand Duke's desk and inside his butchered copy of The Essays of Montaigne

FURTHER READING

The Rules of Civility by Amor Towles

The Noise of Time by Julian Barnes

Anna Karenina by Leo Tolstoy

City of Thieves by David Benioff

The Master and Margarita by Mikhail Bulgakov

These Foolish Things by Deborah Moggach

The Hotel New Hampshire by John Irving

Life: A User's Manual by Georges Perec

BIBLIOGRAPHY

Amor Towles. *A Gentleman in Moscow*, Penguin, 2016

Ron Charles. 'A Gentleman in Moscow is a charming reminder of what it means to be classy.' *The Washington Post*, 19 September 2016

Michelle Dean. 'Amor Towles: A Gentleman in New York.' *Los Angeles Times*, 13 February 2017

Vera Kean. 'Banished to Luxury: Amor Towles.' Publisher's Weekly, 8 July 2016

Craig Taylor, 'A Count Becomes a Waiter in a Novel of Soviet Supremacy.' *The New York Times*, the 23 September 2016

Annalisa Quinn. 'A Gentleman in Moscow is a Grand Hotel Adventure.' *NPR Books*, 3 September 2016

Ryan Vlastelica 'A Gentleman in Moscow is a worthy update to the "great Russian novel." *A.V. Club*, 19 September 2016

Cameron Woodhead. 'A Gentleman in Moscow review: Amor Towles' charming argument for courtesy.' *The Sydney Morning Herald*, 20 January 2017

www.amortowles.com/

www.history.com/topics/russian-revolution

www.gulaghistory.org/

FURTHER TITLES IN THIS SERIES

The Book Thief (Markus Zusak): A Guide for Book Clubs

The Fault in Our Stars (John Green): A Guide for Book Clubs

Frankenstein (Mary Shelley): A Guide for Book Clubs

The Girl on the Train (Paula Hawkins): A Guide for Book Clubs

Go Set a Watchman (Harper Lee): A Guide for Readers

A God in Ruins (Kate Atkinson): A Guide for Book Clubs

The Goldfinch (Donna Tartt): A Guide for Book Clubs

Gone Girl (Gillian Flynn): A Guide for Book Clubs

The Great Gatsby (F. Scott Fitzgerald): A Guide for Book Clubs

The Grownup (Gillian Flynn): A Guide for Book Clubs

The Guernsey Literary and Potato Peel Pie Society (Mary Ann Shaffer & Annie Burrows): A Guide for Book Clubs

The Heart Goes Last (Margaret Atwood): A Guide for Book Clubs

The Husband's Secret (Liane Moriarty): A Guide for Book Clubs

I Know Why the Caged Bird Sings (Maya Angelou): A Guide for Book Clubs

The Light between Oceans (M.L. Stedman): A Guide for Book Clubs

My Brilliant Friend (Elena Ferrante): A Guide for Book Clubs

My Name is Lucy Barton (Elizabeth Strout): A Guide for Book

Clubs

The Narrow Road to the Deep North (Richard Flanagan): A Guide for Book Clubs

The Paying Guests (Sarah Waters): A Guide for Book Clubs

The Secret History (Donna Tartt): A Guide for Book Clubs

The Storied Life of A.J. Fikry (Gabrielle Zevin): A Guide for Book Clubs

The Sympathizer (Viet Thanh Nguyen): A Guide for Book Clubs

The Underground Railroad (Colson Whitehead): A Guide for Book Clubs

ABOUT THE AUTHOR

Kathryn Cope graduated in English Literature from Manchester University and obtained her master's degree in contemporary fiction from the University of York. She is a reviewer and author of The Reading Room Book Group Guides. She lives in the Peak District with her husband and son.

www.amazon.com/author/kathryncope

49695723R00059

Made in the USA
San Bernardino, CA
01 June 2017